An Analysis of

C. L. R. James's

The Black Jacobins
Toussaint L'Ouverture and
the San Domingo Revolution

Nick Broten

Published by Macat International Ltd
24:13 Coda Centre, 189 Munster Road, London SW6 6AW.

Distributed exclusively by Routledge
2 Park Square, Milton Park, Abingdon, Oxon OX14 4RN
711 Third Avenue, New York, NY 10017, USA

Routledge is an imprint of the Taylor & Francis Group, an informa business

www.macat.com
info@macat.com

Cataloguing in Publication Data
A catalogue record for this book is available from the British Library.
Library of Congress Cataloguing-in-Publication Data is available upon request.
Cover illustration: Capucine Deslouis

ISBN 978-1-912302-65-9 (hardback)
ISBN 978-1-912128-89-1 (paperback)
ISBN 978-1-912281-53-4 (e-book)

Notice

CONTENTS

THE MACAT LIBRARY

The Macat Library is a series of unique academic explorations of seminal works in the humanities and social sciences – books and papers that have had a significant and widely recognised impact on their disciplines. It has been created to serve as much more than just a summary of what lies between the covers of a great book. It illuminates and explores the influences on, ideas of, and impact of that book. Our goal is to offer a learning resource that encourages critical thinking and fosters a better, deeper understanding of important ideas.

Each publication is divided into three Sections: Influences, Ideas, and Impact. Each Section has four Modules. These explore every important facet of the work, and the responses to it.

This Section-Module structure makes a Macat Library book easy to use, but it has another important feature. Because each Macat book is written to the same format, it is possible (and encouraged!) to cross-reference multiple Macat books along the same lines of inquiry or research. This allows the reader to open up interesting interdisciplinary pathways.

To further aid your reading, lists of glossary terms and people mentioned are included at the end of this book (these are indicated by an asterisk [*] throughout) – as well as a list of works cited.

Macat has worked with the University of Cambridge to identify the elements of critical thinking and understand the ways in which six different skills combine to enable effective thinking.
Three allow us to fully understand a problem; three more give us the tools to solve it. Together, these six skills make up the **PACIER** model of critical thinking. They are:

ANALYSIS – understanding how an argument is built
EVALUATION – exploring the strengths and weaknesses of an argument
INTERPRETATION – understanding issues of meaning

CREATIVE THINKING – coming up with new ideas and fresh connections
PROBLEM-SOLVING – producing strong solutions
REASONING – creating strong arguments

To find out more, visit **WWW.MACAT.COM.**

CRITICAL THINKING AND *THE BLACK JACOBINS*

Primary critical thinking skill: PROBLEM-SOLVING
Secondary critical thinking skill: CREATIVE THINKING

Today we take it for granted that history is much more than the story of great men and the elites from which they spring. Other forms of history – the histories of gender, class, rebellion and nonconformity – add much-needed context and color to our understanding of the past. But this has not always been so. In CLR James's *The Black Jacobins*, we have one of the earliest, and most defining, examples of how 'history from below' ought to be written.

James's approach is based on his need to resolve two central problems: to understand why the Haitian slave revolt was the only example of a successful slave rebellion in history, and also to grasp the ways in which its history was intertwined with the history of the French Revolution. The book's originality, and its value, rests on its author's ability to ask and answer productive questions of this sort, and in the creativity with which he proved able to generate new hypotheses as a result. As any enduring work of history must be, *The Black Jacobins* is rooted in sound archival research – but its true greatness lies in the originality of James's approach.

ABOUT THE AUTHOR OF THE ORIGINAL WORK

C. L. R. James (1901–89) was born on the Caribbean island of Trinidad, then a British colony, where his father was a schoolteacher. During his career he lived in a number of countries and was variously a journalist, historian, philosopher, playwright, and activist. James was a committed Marxist, siding with the minority Trotskyist branch of the communist movement, and an influential supporter of pan-Africanism, the movement in favor of the political union of all African people. He lived in the United States, but was deported in 1953 for his communist views, although he returned in 1968. Noted both for his devotion to cricket and for his vast influence on the burgeoning field of post-colonial studies, James eventually settled in England, dying in London at the age of 88.

ABOUT THE AUTHOR OF THE ANALYSIS

Nick Broten was educated at the California Institute of Technology and the London School of Economics. He is doing postgraduate work at the Pardee RAND Graduate School and works as an assistant policy analyst at RAND. His current policy interests include designing distribution methods for end-of-life care, closing labour market skill gaps, and understanding biases in risk-taking by venture capitalists.

ABOUT MACAT

GREAT WORKS FOR CRITICAL THINKING

Macat is focused on making the ideas of the world's great thinkers accessible and comprehensible to everybody, everywhere, in ways that promote the development of enhanced critical thinking skills.

It works with leading academics from the world's top universities to produce new analyses that focus on the ideas and the impact of the most influential works ever written across a wide variety of academic disciplines. Each of the works that sit at the heart of its growing library is an enduring example of great thinking. But by setting them in context – and looking at the influences that shaped their authors, as well as the responses they provoked – Macat encourages readers to look at these classics and game-changers with fresh eyes. Readers learn to think, engage and challenge their ideas, rather than simply accepting them.

WAYS IN TO THE TEXT

KEY POINTS

- C. L. R. James (1901–89) was a prolific and influential Trinidadian journalist, historian, playwright, and scholar.

- *The Black Jacobins* documents history's only successful slave revolt: the Haitian Revolution* of 1791 to 1803.

- Offering a historical account from the perspective of a marginalized people (the slaves* of the island of San Domingo,* as Haiti was known in the colonial* period), the book is a striking example of "history from below."*

Who Was C. L. R. James?

The author of *The Black Jacobins: Toussaint L'Ouverture and the San Domingo Revolution* (1938), Cyril Lionel Robert James, was born in 1901 on the Caribbean island of Trinidad, then a British colony. His father was a schoolteacher. A bright child, in 1910 he was awarded a place at a boarding school on the island at the age of nine; this propelled him on a course of scholarship.

James's career as a writer spanned several domains and countries. In the early 1930s he was a sports columnist for the British *Manchester Guardian* newspaper, primarily covering cricket,* while writing plays, short stories, and political history. James was a committed Marxist* and published a history of the communist* movement in 1937, a year before the publication of *The Black Jacobins*. ("Marxism" is named for the political and social analysis of the German economist and political philosopher Karl Marx,* a figure foundational for communist thought; communism seeks to take industry and trade into public ownership with the aim of abolishing social class and, eventually, private property.)

Much of James's work was motivated by his political leanings; in particular, James identified with the Trotskyist* arm of the communist movement rather than with the position taken by Joseph Stalin,* then the leader of the Soviet Union.* Official Soviet policy was that the communist movement should strengthen itself in Russia (where communists had established a government in 1917) and then expand, a policy formulated by Stalin and known as "socialism in one country"; conversely, Trotskyists argued for the incitement of ongoing communist revolutions around the world.

James spent two long periods during his life in the United States, first from 1938 to 1953, and again from 1968. The first of these stays ended when James was deported for his communist views. In the 1980s James moved to London, where he died in 1989.

What Does *The Black Jacobins* Say?

The Black Jacobins was published in 1938. It is a history of the slave revolt in what is today Haiti, then the French colony of San Domingo, that took place between 1791 and 1803; as far as we can determine, it was the only successful revolt by slaves against their masters. The book's title is a reference to the radical political faction known as the Jacobins,* who played a significant role in the French Revolution* of 1789–99 as one of the earliest groups to oppose the monarchy.* A key theme of *The Black Jacobins* is the relationship between the uprising in Paris and the revolt that followed two years later in San Domingo; James weaves the two revolutions together throughout the book.

Much of the emotional power of James's book is established in the opening chapters, in which James describes conditions in San

Domingo in the late eighteenth century. Slavery was central to the island's culture and economy, and a complex social order grew out of it. At the bottom of this hierarchy were the slaves, who existed in conditions of "unceasing brutality."[1] Above the slaves in the hierarchy were "free blacks" and above them lighter-skinned blacks known as mulattos*—people of mixed race. As James notes, "The free blacks, comparatively speaking, were not many, and so despised was the black skin that even a mulatto slave felt himself superior to the free black man."[2] In the white population, the island was ruled by what James calls "big whites," including merchants and planters. They were above the "small whites," who were the "small lawyers, the notaries, the clerks, the artisans, the grocers."[3]

The first of the slave revolts in Haiti began in 1791, and James describes the effort as a "thoroughly prepared and organized mass movement."[4] The early revolutionaries murdered their masters and burnt down the plantations where they had worked. In James's narrative, however, these early revolts only became a revolution under the leadership of Toussaint L'Ouverture,* a former slave who emerged as a leader of the revolt in 1792. L'Ouverture is the central character in *The Black Jacobins* and the book is in many ways a celebration of his leadership—James repeatedly states how instrumental L'Ouverture was to the revolt's final success.

The revolt that L'Ouverture led was neither swift nor simple; he and his supporters defeated the landowners in San Domingo and repelled attacks from France, Britain, and Spain. In the end, slavery was abolished and the Republic of Haiti was established. For James, this revolution was the beginning of the regional identity of the West Indies* (the islands of the Caribbean Sea) and provoked thoughts of revolution across the region. In an appendix to *The Black Jacobins* first published in 1963, James links L'Ouverture's leadership in Haiti to the leadership of Fidel Castro,* leader of the 1953 revolution in Cuba:* "The people who made them [the revolutions], the problems and the attempts to solve them, are peculiarly West Indian, the product of a peculiar origin and a peculiar history."[5]

Why Does *The Black Jacobins* Matter?

The Black Jacobins is a central text in the history of the Caribbean, and an early and seminal example of what is known as "history from below." The book has inspired many interpretations and has been used both as a key work of history and a rallying cry for freedom from oppression; it remains the definitive account of the revolution in Haiti.

Readers of the book will be exposed to a relatively unknown but deeply important moment in history—a revolution sometimes overshadowed by similar events in France and the United States. Students will also be confronted with questions about the nature of revolution that remain relevant today. For example, James's narrative relies heavily on the ingenuity and leadership ability of L'Ouverture, a man who, in James's telling, shaped history to his will. Today's students, and particularly those with an interest in politics and social action, will benefit from considering the different factors that shape social movements, including the influence of great leaders and the environments in which they develop.

More broadly, *The Black Jacobins* will challenge students to think critically about history. According to the global financial institution the World Bank, today Haiti is one of the poorest nations in the world and its history of colonialism (being possessed and exploited by foreign nations), slavery, and independence remains very important in understanding its current political, economic, and social conditions. *The Black Jacobins* celebrates the intelligence, boldness, and righteousness of the revolutionaries. This tension—between the optimism prompted by Toussaint's revolution over oppression and the problems on the island today—raises a number of questions. We might ask what went wrong between then and now, and if Haiti's present poverty is due to it being excluded from the international community after the revolution. The book is a useful starting point in the search for answers.

Kenan Malik,* an English author who writes on matters of race, culture, and biology, refers to this tension when he writes of the optimism, even naïvety, in the book: "Today, in an age of cynicism and disillusionment, in which the idea of social transformation seems illusory, and in which the very state of contemporary Haiti seems to question James's vision, that vision, it seems to me, is more important than ever, an aspiration to be celebrated, not denigrated."[6]

NOTES

1   C. L. R. James, *The Black Jacobins: Toussaint L'Ouverture and the San Domingo Revolution* (New York: Vintage Books, 1989), 15.

2   James, *Black Jacobins*, 43.

3   James, *Black Jacobins*, 33.

4   James, *Black Jacobins*, 86.

5   James, *Black Jacobins*, 391.

6   Kenan Malik, "C. L. R. James: The Black Jacobins," Kenan Malik, August 17, 2010, accessed November 13, 2015, http://www.kenanmalik.com/reviews/james_jacobins.html.

SECTION 1
INFLUENCES

THE AUTHOR AND THE HISTORICAL CONTEXT

KEY POINTS

- *The Black Jacobins* is a fascinating history of a relatively unknown but very important event—the world's only successful slave* uprising.

- In the course of his life, James was a cricket* reporter, historian, and political activist.

- James lived during several important events, including the Russian Revolution* of 1917, both World War I and II,* and the rise of communism.* His leftist political views come through in his book, a work of "history from below"* presenting the Haitian Revolution* from the viewpoint of the slaves.

Why Read This Text?

C. L. R. James's *The Black Jacobins: Toussaint L'Ouverture and the San Domingo Revolution* (1938) is a riveting, powerful, and definitive history of one of the most important but under-recognized events in history: the slave revolution in what is now known as Haiti from 1791 to 1803. The book is important not only as a historical account of the event, but as one of the first examples of history told from the point of view of an oppressed population, in this case the slaves of the island. James, a politically engaged journalist from Trinidad, spends considerable time in the book discussing the awful conditions of slavery in San Domingo* (as Haiti was then known) before revolution, and the remarkable leadership qualities of the slave-turned-revolutionary Toussaint L'Ouverture.* James's outlook—he was influenced by

> ❝ The revolt is the only successful slave revolt in history, and the odds it had to overcome is evidence of the magnitude of the interests that were involved. ❞
>
> C. L. R. James, *The Black Jacobins: Toussaint L'Ouverture and the San Domingo Revolution*

Marxist* philosophy (the historical and social analysis of the German political philosopher Karl Marx*), and was a native of the Caribbean island of Trinidad—distinguishes the book from other accounts of the Haitian Revolution.

Beyond this bottom-up history (that is, history told from the perspective of the marginalized, rather than those of high status or political influence), readers of *The Black Jacobins* will gain a greater understanding of the political dynamics of the late eighteenth century. This includes not only the events in San Domingo but the influence of the revolutions in America* and France,* and the key role slavery played in these politics. From the book's unflinching description of slavery, readers will gain a fuller appreciation of the barbarity of that practice and the nature of the economies that were built from it. As a radical work, *The Black Jacobins* will appeal to readers who lean towards revolutionary politics—but it is also a work engaging to a wider audience.

Author's Life

C. L. R. James was born in 1901 in Trinidad, at the time a British colony. James wore many professional hats in the course of his life, from journalist, historian, and philosopher, to playwright and activist. His life overlapped with many significant events, and James seems to have had an ability to be in the right place at the right time. As the *New York Times* notes in his obituary, referencing the pan-Africanist* movement that sought solidarity between African nations for the sake of economic and social advancement, "James, known always by his initials, debated Marcus Garvey* in England, confronted [the Russian revolutionary communist] Trotsky* in Mexico, helped conceive pan-Africanism and influenced leaders of African revolutions including Kwame Nkrumah* of Ghana."[1]

At the age of nine, James won a scholarship to Queens Royal College, a Trinidadian boarding school; on graduating, he became a schoolteacher. In 1932, he traveled to England with the intention of working as a writer, an ambition he fulfilled as a cricket* correspondent for the *Manchester Guardian*, a leading British newspaper. While in England he was involved in revolutionary politics, and much of his writing from the period reveals a growing Marxist influence. In 1938 James moved to the United States, where he lived until being deported in 1953 during the crackdown on communist* activity known as McCarthyism* after the politician Joseph McCarthy, the US senator who authored the anti-communist legislation that characterized the period. In 1968, James was allowed to return to the United States, where he taught at Federal City College, now the University of the District of Columbia, in Washington, DC.

At the time of his death in 1989, James lived in London.

Author's Background

James's life coincided with a number of great events in political and economic history, including the 1917 Russian Revolution, in which Russia became a communist state, World War I and II, the catastrophic economic downturn of the 1930s known as the Great Depression,* and the end of the period of European colonialism* of Africa, the Caribbean, and Asia. Most importantly, James's early life was a time of great revolutionary feeling. Though it may be difficult to understand today, James wrote *The Black Jacobins* at a time of competing revolutionary ideas—the international communist movement was considered a genuine threat to capitalism* (the social and economic

17

system dominant in the West, and increasingly throughout the developing world) and freedom; the rise of the extreme right-wing ideology of fascism* was seen as a reaction to the rise of communism. James discussed this tension in his 1937 book *World Revolution 1917–1936*, noting, "With every failure of the Left the Right increases its audacity."[2]

Understanding the nature of revolution and its role in history was not, therefore, a purely academic exercise for James. To give an indication of the contemporary political environment, in 1934 Leon Trotsky* (one of the two leaders of the Russian Revolution, along with Lenin*) published the pamphlet "If America Should Go Communist," in which he predicts the nature of the country after a communist revolution: "The American soviet government will take firm possession of the commanding heights of your business system: the banks, the key industries and the transportation and communication systems. It will then give the farmers, the small tradespeople and businessmen a good long time to think things over and see how well the nationalized section of industry is working."[3]

Though *The Black Jacobins* depicts events of the late eighteenth century, it is clearly a work of the 1930s.

NOTES

1 C. Gerald Fraser, "C. L. R. James, Historian, Critic and Pan-Africanist, is Dead at 88," *New York Times*, June 2, 1989, , accessed January 21, 2016, http://www.nytimes.com/1989/06/02/obituaries/c-l-r-james-historian-critic-and-pan-africanist-is-dead-at-88.html?_r=0.

2 C. L. R. James, "After Hitler, Our Turn," in *World Revolution 1917–1936*, *Marxists*, accessed November 13, 2015, https://www.marxists.org/archive/james-clr/works/world/ch12.htm.

3 Leon Trotsky, "If America Should Go Communist," August 1934, accessed November 13, 2015, https://www.marxists.org/archive/trotsky/1934/08/ame.htm.

ACADEMIC CONTEXT

KEY POINTS

- *The Black Jacobins* is influenced by the Marxist* approach to history, which views history as basically driven by economic forces.

- James's book finds its roots in the work of the Italian political philosopher Antonio Gramsci,* who developed the theory of cultural hegemony,* according to which the dominant class in society has a big influence over both economy and culture.

- James found inspiration from his immediate surroundings in London in writing *The Black Jacobins*, including his work with the African American singer and political activist Paul Robeson.*

The Work in its Context

C. L. R. James's *The Black Jacobins: Toussaint L'Ouverture and the San Domingo Revolution* is an early example of "history from below"*— although the term itself, denoting works of history told from the perspective of people of low social and economic status, only began to be used by historians long after *The Black Jacobins* was published in 1938. James's book was one of several works that inspired the field of subaltern,* or postcolonial,* studies. Historians from this branch of social inquiry, which deals with the various legacies of the colonial* period, write history from the point of view of the "subalterns"— those groups that have been excluded from traditional power structures and opportunities—such as slaves* and poor peasants.

James's approach to history, and indeed the whole of the subaltern school, cannot be understood without appreciating the work of Karl

> ❝ Men make their own history, but they do not make it as they please; they do not make it under self-selected circumstances, but under circumstances existing already, given and transmitted from the past. The tradition of all dead generations weighs like a nightmare on the brains of the living. ❞
> Karl Marx, *The Eighteenth Brumaire of Louis Bonaparte*

Marx,* whose idea of history was shaped by the German philosopher G.W. F. Hegel's* notion of the dialectic:* a word denoting the tension created between an idea or concept and the reaction that rises up in opposition to it; this "antithesis" eventually leads to a "synthesis"—a fusion of the two. Karl Marx built on this idea to develop his notion of historical materialism,* according to which history is pushed forward by economic forces. The word "materialism" here should not be confused with its contemporary meaning, a focus on material possessions. Rather, Marx believed the driving force of history was how the means of production* (the tools and resources used to produce goods and services) are owned and organized in any society. For example, in a capitalist* economy, most economic activity is in private hands, and businesses act in a way that promote the profits and interests of their owners. As Marx writes in *The German Ideology*, "This mode of production must not be considered simply as being the production of the physical existence of the individuals. Rather it is a definite form of activity of these individuals, a definite form of expressing their life, a definite mode of life on their part. As individuals express their life, so they are."[1]

In other words, Marx believed that individuals tended to see the world according to their role within the means of production—as business owners, for example, or wage earners. The interests of those often-competing groups is what drives history, according to this view.

Overview of the Field

Antonio Gramsci extended Marx's theory to the discussion of culture, and in so doing laid the groundwork for subaltern history, or history from below. Put simply, Gramsci developed a theory of cultural hegemony stating that the dominant social class, for example the bourgeoisie* (business owners), not only had a big influence over the economy, but over a society's culture as well. Gramsci believed that the creation of an alternative, or proletarian* culture—that is, a culture of the workers, promoting revolutionary ideas—was necessary for the overthrow of capitalism and the rise of a communist* state.

To some extent, this is also the goal of subaltern studies, of which *The Black Jacobins* plays a very early part. Subaltern studies represent the history of groups excluded from the dominant culture. As the Indian historian Dipesh Chakrabarty* writes, "Both subaltern studies and the 'history from below' school were Marxist in inspiration; both owed a certain intellectual debt to the Italian communist Antonio Gramsci in trying to move away from deterministic, Stalinist* readings of Marx. The word 'subaltern' itself—and, of course, the well-known concept of 'hegemony' so critical to the theoretical project of subaltern studies—go back to the writings of Gramsci."[2] ("Determinism" here is the idea that certain outcomes arrive as an inevitable result of certain facts or states.)

Due to the similarity between Gramsci's concept of culture and the way in which James discussed marginalized groups throughout his life as a writer, the two are often associated. It is important to note, however, that on strict ideological grounds—specifically Marxist—their views are not identical.

Academic Influences

While James was strongly influenced by a Marxist approach to history, *The Black Jacobins* is not rooted in any academic school or debate. It emerged, rather, from the tense political environment of the late 1930s.

C. L. R. James was a keen observer of both political events and cultural developments, and there is some evidence that the author was inspired by his immediate surroundings in London, while writing *The Black Jacobins*. The historian Robert Hill* says the tone of the book was influenced by the author's relationship with Paul Robeson, a leading African American singer and actor who acted in James's play about the Haitian Revolution:* "At a very profound and fundamental level, Robeson as a man *shattered* James's colonial conception of the Black Physique. In its place the magnificent stature of Robeson gave to him a new appreciation of the powerful and extraordinary capacities which the African possessed, in both head and body."[3]

According to Hill, Robeson helped James abandon the "unconscious prototype" that black West Indians grew up with of seeing white people, rather than black people, as the peak of physical beauty. James, however, challenged this view in a manuscript for his never-published autobiography: "Hill is quite wrong when he says that Robeson shattered my West Indian* conception of physical personality. We had people taking part from Guyana in Olympic Games* and winning."[4] Still, James accepts that powerful black figures played a role in reshaping his understanding of history.

NOTES

1 Karl Marx, *The German Ideology* (written 1845–6, published 1932), *Marxists*, accessed November 13, 2015, https://www.marxists.org/archive/marx/works/1845/german-ideology/ch01a.htm.

2 Dipesh Chakrabarty, "Subaltern Studies and Postcolonial Historiography," *Nepantla: Views from South* 1, no.1 (2000): 14.

3 Robert A. Hill, "In England, 1932–38," in *C. L. R. James: His Life and Work*, ed. Paul Buhle (London: Allison & Busby, 1986), 73.

4 C. L. R. James's papers, boxes 2 and 5, Rare Book & Manuscript Library, Columbia University Library, New York.

THE PROBLEM

KEY POINTS

- The core question of *The Black Jacobins* is how slaves* in San Domingo*—as the island of Haiti was then known— managed to achieve their freedom.

- James consulted numerous historical accounts of the events in San Domingo, including primary sources (original documents), histories in French and English, and travel books.

- Although James was not engaged directly in the day's academic debate on the Haitian Revolution* when he conceived and wrote *The Black Jacobins*, he did reference several French historians of the French Revolution* as influences.

Core Question

C. L. R. James asks a central question in *The Black Jacobins: Toussaint L'Ouverture and the San Domingo Revolution*: How did a group of uneducated slaves in what is today Haiti successfully overthrow their colonial* masters and defeat the invasions that followed from France, Britain, and Spain? As the only successful slave revolt in history, the events in San Domingo warrant attention. As a historian, James's aim is to describe the slave revolt from the point of view of the revolutionaries and their leader, Toussaint L'Ouverture.*

Throughout James's historical investigation, however, he is asking another question: What is the nature of revolution, and what are the conditions in which the proletariat* (the workers) can overthrow those responsible for their oppression? Although James does not explicitly frame his discussion in these terms, his political viewpoint

> ❝ The writer has sought not only to analyze, but to demonstrate in their movement, the economic forces of the age; their molding of society and politics, of men in the mass and individual men; the powerful reaction of these on their environment at one of those rare moments when society is at boiling point and therefore fluid. ❞
>
> C. L. R. James, *The Black Jacobins: Toussaint L'Ouverture and the San Domingo Revolution*

informs his discussion of history. James's Marxist* beliefs also place the book squarely at the heart of the political conflicts of the late 1930s. As he writes, "The violent conflicts of our age enable our practiced vision to see into the very bones of previous revolutions more easily than heretofore."[1] He refers to the violent upheavals going on across Europe at the time—the eve of World War II.* He notes the revolt led by Spain's fascist* leader when he writes of "Franco's* heavy artillery," and refers to the mass repression in the Soviet Union* when he writes of the "rattle of Stalin's* firing squads … Such is our age and this book is of it, with something of the fever and the fret."[2]

The Participants

As a work of history, *The Black Jacobins* builds upon previous works on the revolution in San Domingo and the conditions there more generally, much of it published in French. These works include scholarly histories, first-person accounts, official archives, and travel books. James provides an annotated bibliography of these works in the book, in which he writes, "Despite the importance and interest of the subject, it was for long difficult to find in English or French a comprehensive treatment of the San Domingo revolution … Both in insight and objectivity the Haitian writers are easily the best."[3]

James draws on a long list of sources—notably Colonel Henri de Poyen-Bellisle's 1899 *Histoire Militaire de la Révolution de Saint-Domingue* (A Military History of the Revolution of San Domingo). James writes,"This is the official French account. Poyen misunderstands the whole campaign, both the offensive plan of Leclerc* and the defensive plan of Toussaint … there is no limit to the brazenness of these imperialist historians."[4] Despite disagreeing with Poyen's version of history, he finds him to be a "careful, scholarly writer" and is able to build on his work.[5] This is a theme in James's work—though he frequently disagrees with the work of scholars before him, he finds that he can use their work in his own.

The Contemporary Debate

In writing *The Black Jacobins*, James was not responding to previous points of view on the topic, though he does reference the work of others throughout. In an important way, James's history of the Haitian Revolution builds on the work of the scholars of another revolt that started barely two years earlier, the French Revolution. As he notes, "It is impossible to understand the San Domingo revolution unless it is studied in close relationship with the revolution in France. Fortunately the French historical school of the French Revolution is one of the greatest historical schools of Western civilization."[6]

James lists several French historians who inspired his own study. They exposed the economic foundations of the French Revolution, wrote about the personalities of its main actors, and covered the politics of the period. James credits these influences in the book: "I have sought all through to show the direct influence of the [French] Revolution on events and leading personalities in San Domingo."[7] It appears from James's biography that his awareness of and interest in this history was sparked when he moved to Europe in the 1930s. In that sense, the intellectual basis of the work is James's attempt to unify his understanding of West Indian* culture—that is, the culture of the islands of the Caribbean Sea—and history with the debates over history and politics going on at the time in England and France.

NOTES

1 C. L. R. James, *The Black Jacobins: Toussaint L'Ouverture and the San Domingo Revolution* (New York: Vintage Books, 1989), xi.

2 James, *Black Jacobins*, xi.

3 James, *Black Jacobins*, 381.

4 James, *Black Jacobins*, 382.

5 James, *Black Jacobins*, 382.

6 James, *Black Jacobins*, 383.

7 James, *Black Jacobins*, 385.

THE AUTHOR'S CONTRIBUTION

KEY POINTS

- James had several goals in writing *The Black Jacobins*, from describing the first successful slave* revolt to understanding revolution more generally.

- James bases his analysis on archival work and previous historical works.

- *The Black Jacobins* is a unique work for the way it weaves together the Haitian Revolution* and the French Revolution.*

Author's Aims

C. L. R. James's primary objective in writing *The Black Jacobins: Toussaint L'Ouverture and the San Domingo Revolution* was to explain why and how the only successful slave revolution in history occurred.[1] His goals extended beyond that, however, as noted by the writer Brian Meeks:* "James had at least five objectives in mind. First, the successful Haitian revolutionary struggle was to be used as a tool to teach a new generation of anti-colonialists … Second, James hoped to expose what he saw as the [plots] of the colonial*/imperial* powers …Third, while using a West Indian* study to draw lessons for the African continent, he also sought to highlight the particular role of the West Indies in world history … Fourth, he sought to explore the characteristics and dynamics of revolution … And fifth, he sought to demonstrate the usefulness and effectiveness of a certain interpretation of Marxist* methodology in the analysis and understanding of history."[2]

James's narrative of the revolution is directly chronological, with occasional asides to discuss the context of the politics. In the first three

> ❝ The transformation of slaves, trembling in hundreds before a single white man, into a powerful people able to organize themselves and defeat the most powerful European nations of their day, is one of the great epics of revolutionary struggle and achievement. ❞
>
> C. L. R. James, *The Black Jacobins: Toussaint L'Ouverture and the San Domingo Revolution*

chapters, he discusses the conditions on the island of San Domingo* (present-day Haiti) before the revolution. Then the story unfolds, with chapter titles indicating the evolution of events: "The San Domingo Masses Begin" describes the early unrest; "And the Paris Masses Complete" connects the unrest in San Domingo to the French Revolution and discusses the complex allegiances of the San Domingo revolutionaries; "The Rise of Toussaint" introduces L'Ouverture* as the main leader of the revolution; and the chapters that follow describe a series of military conflicts. The final two chapters of the book, "The Bourgeoisie* Prepares to Restore Slavery" and "The War of Independence," describe the final stages of the revolution in which L'Ouverture was finally killed.

Approach

As is the case with any honest history, the basis of James's approach was archival work. Preparing for the book, he consulted several archives in France, Haiti, and Britain. He states that the French National Archives, which include "many thousands of official reports and private letters dealing with the whole period from 1789 to 1804," were most important.[3] Importantly, James "does not claim to have examined these archives exhaustively … but much of the ground has been covered by other writers."[4]

James manages to turn his historical work into a story in which it is sometimes difficult to differentiate between his opinions and what is taken from the archives; he frequently gives characters thoughts and psychological motivations. For example, he writes, "Occupied with his European campaigns, [the French military leader Napoleon] Bonaparte* never lost sight of San Domingo, as he never lost sight of anything."[5] In another example, he writes, "Maitland, a prejudiced Englishman, did not think L'Ouverture very intelligent. But Maitland had seen that the blacks in San Domingo, now that they had military experience, organization and leaders, were a match for any European expedition."[6] In both examples it is unclear whether James directly read these thoughts in documents in the archives or simply attributed them to these historical characters.

Contribution in Context

The way in which James weaves together the slave revolt in San Domingo with the revolution in France makes the book unique. The result is a fascinating description of the roots of a revolution. He looks to France and the revolt of August 10, 1792 in which the monarchy* was overthrown, writing, "What has all this to do with the slaves? Everything. The workers and peasants of France could not have been expected to take any interest in the colonial question in normal times, any more than one can expect similar interests from British or French workers today. But now they were roused. They were striking at royalty, tyranny, reaction, and oppression of all types, and with these they included slavery."

Another innovative feature of *The Black Jacobins* is James's telling of history from the point of view of slaves. With his worldly outlook, he is uniquely able to connect the characters in this story, and particularly Toussaint L'Ouverture, to famous figures of European and American history. Referencing revolutionaries and political philosophers from ancient Greece to the United States of the early-nineteenth century, he writes, "Pericles,* Thomas Paine,* Thomas Jefferson,* Karl Marx* and Friedrich Engels* were men of a liberal education, formed in the traditions of ethics, philosophy, and history. Toussaint was a slave, not six years out of slavery, bearing alone the unaccustomed burden of war and government, dictating his thoughts in the crude words of a broken dialect."[7]

NOTES

1   C. L. R. James, *The Black Jacobins: Toussaint L'Ouverture and the San Domingo Revolution* (New York: Vintage Books, 1989), ix.

2   Brian Meeks, "Rereading *The Black Jacobins*: James, the Dialectic and the Revolutionary Conjuncture," *Social and Economic Studies* 43, no. 3 (1994): 76.

3   James, *Black Jacobins*, 379.

4   James, *Black Jacobins*, 380.

5   James, *Black Jacobins*, 270.

6   James, *Black Jacobins*, 211.

7   James, *Black Jacobins*, 197.

SECTION 2
IDEAS

MODULE 5
MAIN IDEAS

KEY POINTS

- James tells the story of revolution in San Domingo,* first describing conditions on the island in vivid detail.

- The slave* revolt of 1791–1803 was inspired by the French Revolution* of 1789–99.

- While the book is clearly written and free of jargon, some knowledge of European history and geography will help readers to follow the story.

Key Themes

In *The Black Jacobins: Toussaint L'Ouverture and the San Domingo Revolution*, C. L. R. James tells the story of the Haitian Revolution,* which took place from 1791 to 1803, from the viewpoint of the black slaves of the colony, then known as San Domingo.

James's analysis of the events builds on a rich description of the social conditions on the island before the revolution; he presents the social conditions that led to the revolution in dialectical* terms— according to which a given situation (in this case, the brutal exploitation of the slaves) led to an opposing reaction (the slave revolt) that spurred a further reaction (efforts by the local and European authorities to put down the uprising), and so on. James frames his story in terms of the struggle between what he labels "The Property" (the slaves) and "The Owners." He helps the reader comprehend the turbulent environment of the period with description, such as this account of the awful conditions that slaves endured in transit from West Africa to the Caribbean: "On the ships the slaves were packed in the hold on galleries one above another …

> ❝ In a revolution, when the ceaseless slow accumulation of centuries bursts into volcanic eruption, the meteoric flares and flights above are a meaningless chaos and lend themselves to infinite caprice and romanticism unless the observer sees them always as projections of the subsoil from which they came. ❞
>
> C. L. R. James, *The Black Jacobins: Toussaint L'Ouverture and the San Domingo Revolution*

The close proximity of so many naked human beings, their bruised and festering flesh, the fetid air, the prevailing dysentery, the accumulation of filth, turned these holds into a hell."[1]

In reference to "The Owners," James identifies three groups: the "San Domingo planters, British bourgeoisie* (business owners), and French bourgeoisie," the most important of whom were the planters, who directed the growing of sugar, coffee, and other crops, which were the source of the colony's wealth.[2]

James describes San Domingo in the late eighteenth century as a violent and morally degenerate place, with "gambling-dens (for everyone in San Domingo played and great fortunes were won and lost in a few days), dance halls, and private brothels."[3] Slavery was the foundation of the local economy. As James writes, referring to "small whites," or those at the bottom of the white economic food chain, "No small white was a servant, no white man did any work that he could not get a Negro to do for him."[4] In contrast to these small whites, "big whites" included wealthy merchants, plantation owners, and "agents of the maritime bourgeoisie."[5] Occupying an awkward middle position between these groups were people of mixed racial heritage, known as mulattos,* who considered themselves to be superior to the slaves and were at times their opponents.

Exploring the Ideas

Having established the context for revolution—a small island built around the institution of slavery—James describes the events. In brief, he portrays the revolution as follows: "In August 1791, after two years of the French Revolution and its repercussions in San Domingo, the slaves revolted. The struggle lasted for 12 years. The slaves defeated in turn the local whites and the soldiers of the French monarchy,* a Spanish invasion, a British expedition of some 60,000 men, and a French expedition of similar size under [Napoleon] Bonaparte's* brother-in-law. The defeat of Bonaparte's expedition in 1803 resulted in the establishment of the Negro state of Haiti which has lasted to this day."[6]

The connection between the ideals of the slaves in San Domingo and the revolutionaries in France is central to the book. Indeed, James presents the Haitian Revolution as the purest example of the themes of the French Revolution. James links the events directly: "And meanwhile, what of the slaves? They had heard of the revolution [in France] and had construed it in their own image: the white slaves of France had risen, and killed their masters, and were now enjoying the fruits of the earth. It was gravely inaccurate in fact, but they had caught the spirit of the thing. Liberty. Equality. Fraternity."[7]

This revolutionary energy, however, did not immediately translate into successful revolution. By July 1792, whites on San Domingo and in France "were still looking upon the slave revolt as a huge riot which would be put down in time, once the division between the slave-owners was closed."[8] To James, the key figure that changed the slave revolt into a deeper revolution was Toussaint L'Ouverture,* the hero of the book.

Language and Expression

The Black Jacobins is clearly and powerfully written. Though James himself was influenced by Marxist* political ideology, his writing is largely free of Marxist terminology, only occasionally referring (for example) to the "bourgeoisie" or "proletariat."* An example is this description of the relations between the social classes in France's revolution: "The rich are only defeated when running for their lives. Inexperienced in revolution, the bourgeoisie had not purged the ministerial offices, where the royalist bureaucrats still sat plotting for the restoration of the royal power."[9] As this quote shows, the tone of the book is somewhat journalistic and James is occasionally conversational. He focuses on events rather than academic concepts.

The most challenging aspect of the book for today's readers will likely be keeping track of the characters in the revolutions in Haiti and France. James does not assume the reader to have prior knowledge of these events, but he does move easily between the two revolutions, and certain readers may miss some of the author's references. Similarly, knowledge of the political events of the late eighteenth century globally, including American and British politics, will help the reader to understand James's message. Finally, readers may want to consult a historical map to understand James's geographical references.

NOTES

1   C. L. R. James, *The Black Jacobins: Toussaint L'Ouverture and the San Domingo Revolution* (New York: Vintage Books, 1989), 8.

2   James, *Black Jacobins*, 27.

3   James, *Black Jacobins*, 32.

4   James, *Black Jacobins*, 33.

5   James, *Black Jacobins*, 33.

6   James, *Black Jacobins*, ix.

7   James, *Black Jacobins*, 81.

8   James, *Black Jacobins*, 117.

9   James, *Black Jacobins*, 78.

MODULE 6
SECONDARY IDEAS

KEY POINTS

- The personality and character of the leader of the Haiti Revolution,* Toussaint L'Ouverture,* is central to the book.

- James describes L'Ouverture as uncommonly intelligent, committed, and idealistic.

- James's departure from Marxist* orthodoxy has been overlooked in discussions of the book.

Other Ideas

While C. L. R. James's *The Black Jacobins: Toussaint L'Ouverture and the San Domingo Revolution* (1938) is mainly concerned with telling the story of the slave* revolution in Haiti, he is equally interested in describing, and to some extent celebrating, the life of Toussaint L'Ouverture, a former slave who became a highly effective military leader in the revolution. In fact, in the preface to the book James writes that "the individual leadership responsible for this unique achievement was almost entirely the work of a single man—Toussaint L'Ouverture." James describes L'Ouverture's rise from slave to military leader with a certain amount of awe. As he says, "Slavery dulls the intellect and degrades the character of the slave. There was nothing of that dullness or degradation in Toussaint."[1] Accordingly, James spends considerable time in the book showing L'Ouverture's rare intelligence, as represented in his writing and military strategy. He says, "The writer believes, and is confident the narrative will prove, that between 1789 and 1815, with the single exception of [Napoleon] Bonaparte* himself, no single figure appeared on the historical stage more greatly gifted than this Negro, a slave till he was 45."[2]

> **❝** The man who so deliberately decided to join the revolution was 45 years of age, an advanced age for those times, grey already, and known to everyone as Old Toussaint. **❞**
>
> C. L. R. James, *The Black Jacobins: Toussaint L'Ouverture and the San Domingo Revolution*

James also makes an effort to show L'Ouverture as someone who took seriously the ideals that drove him to revolution. In this sense, he was a figure of the Enlightenment*—the intellectual movement that began in the seventeenth century that influenced Europe and its colonies to move towards reason, liberty, and tolerance. Writers readily compare L'Ouverture to other revolutionary leaders of the period, including Thomas Jefferson,* the revolutionary leader of the young United States.

Exploring the Ideas

The character of L'Ouverture is one of the most compelling parts of *The Black Jacobins*. James presents him as having exceptional intellectual ability, which enabled L'Ouverture to take on Europe's most sophisticated military leaders. L'Ouverture's father is described as the son of a "petty chieftain in Africa" who was captured in West Africa and "bought by a colonist of some sensibility, who … allowed him a certain liberty on the plantation,"[3] setting him somewhat apart from other slaves. James portrays L'Ouverture in less flattering ways as well, describing him as "very small, ugly, and ill shaped,"[4] although with "eyes like steel and no one ever laughed in his presence."[5] L'Ouverture also gained important experience in the early stages of the slave revolt so that "from the very beginning he maneuvered with uncanny certainty not only between local parties in San Domingo* but between the international forces at work."[6]

The events towards the end of L'Ouverture's life may cast this into question, although James argues that L'Ouverture's later decisions boost his stature. In 1801, he developed a constitution for San Domingo and ruled the territory as an independent state. In response, the French leader Napoleon Bonaparte sent troops to the island with the unstated aim of restoring slavery to the island. Ultimately L'Ouverture returned control of San Domingo to France, which had just gone through its own revolution. Toussaint's decision was based on trust: he "could not believe that the French ruling class would be so depraved, so lost to all sense of decency, as to try to restore slavery."[7] This decision led to the defection of many of Toussaint's generals, the "War of Independence," led chiefly by Jean-Jacques Dessalines* after L'Ouverture's capture in 1802, and ultimately to his death.

As James writes, "The defeat of Toussaint in the War of Independence and his imprisonment and death in Europe are universally looked upon as a tragedy."[8] Still, James states, L'Ouverture remained committed to the shared ideals of the French and Haitian revolutions. His undoing did not come from his abandoning those ideals, but because others who claimed to stand for those ideals abandoned him. "Toussaint's error," James writes, "sprang from the very qualities that made him what he was … Toussaint's failure was the failure of enlightenment, not of darkness."[9]

Overlooked

The Black Jacobins has been studied for some 80 years; little has been overlooked. According to the writer Brian Meeks,* the "aspect of the study, however, on which the least focus has been directed, lies at its very heart. James's methodology, which in form and stated intent is clearly Marxist, nevertheless follows its own peculiar trajectory."[10] Here, Meeks is referring to a tension between the plot of *The Black Jacobins* and traditional ideas of Marxist history. The standard Marxist view is that history is largely driven by economic conditions, and that individuals attempting to change the course of history are limited by history in what they can accomplish. This viewpoint is informed by the notion of historical materialism,* which sees historical progress as the result of fundamentally economic forces.

In a subtle way, *The Black Jacobins* departs from this orthodox approach. As Meeks writes, "In the end James remains a Marxist, but in order to do so, he elevates the individual and agency [that is, the individual's ability to act] to levels unprecedented in classical Marxism."[11] James's celebration of Toussaint L'Ouverture is a striking example of this break from the deterministic view, according to which individuals do not matter much in relation to the unfolding of history. L'Ouverture, James writes, "dominated from his entry until circumstances removed him from the scene. The history of the San Domingo revolution will therefore largely be a record of his achievements and his political personality."[12]

NOTES

1   C. L. R. James, *The Black Jacobins: Toussaint L'Ouverture and the San Domingo Revolution* (New York: Vintage Books, 1989), 91.

2   James, *Black Jacobins*, x.

3   James, *Black Jacobins*, 19.

4   James, *Black Jacobins*, 92.

5   James, *Black Jacobins*, 93.

6   James, *Black Jacobins*, 91.

7   James, *Black Jacobins*, 282.

8   James, *Black Jacobins*, 289.

9   James, *Black Jacobins*, 288.

10 Brian Meeks, "Rereading *The Black Jacobins*: James, the Dialectic and the Revolutionary Conjuncture," *Social and Economic Studies* 43, no. 3 (1994): 77.

11 Meeks, "Rereading," 81.

12 James, *Black Jacobins*, x.

MODULE 7
ACHIEVEMENT

KEY POINTS

- *The Black Jacobins* was successful in depicting the Haitian Revolution* and linking it to broader questions, including the role of revolution and the nature of West Indian* leadership.

- Future events, including revolutions around the world, have done little to change the basic ideas of the book.

- Despite James's revolutionary Marxist* politics and his book's West Indian setting, the work is accessible and valuable across cultures.

Assessing the Argument

C. L. R. James was hugely successful in realizing his goals for *The Black Jacobins: Toussaint L'Ouverture and the San Domingo Revolution*. Not only is it largely unquestioned in terms of historical accuracy, it also touches on wider related issues: the nature of revolution, the particular flavor of revolution in the West Indies, and the role of revolution in historical change. The audience of the book has been broad and engaged, and readers have found it both intellectually and personally inspiring.

In terms of the core question of the book—why and how did the Haitian Revolution occur?—James's answer is both compelling and frustrating. He clearly describes the horrific conditions prior to revolution, and connects the seeds of the Haitian Revolution to the overthrow of the monarchy* in France. Still, much of James's "how" rests on the shoulders of Toussaint L'Ouverture,* the book's central character. It is clear from James's description of the revolution that he believes it would not have been successful without a leader like

> ❝ Great men make history, but only such history as it is possible for them to make. Their freedom of achievement is limited by the necessities of their environment. To portray the limits of those necessities and the realization, complete or partial, of all possibilities, that is the true business of the historian. ❞
>
> C. L. R. James, *The Black Jacobins: Toussaint L'Ouverture and the San Domingo Revolution*

L'Ouverture. He is seeking to show an example of West Indian leadership overcoming great odds. Though there is little in the historical record to contradict this, it is possible that James slightly overstates the importance of L'Ouverture in order to have a great and charismatic character at the center of his story.

Achievement in Context

As *The Black Jacobins* was written more than one hundred years after the events it describes, there have been no serious revisions to the ideas in the book due to new developments coming to light. In fact, it is a tribute to the strength of the book that it has continued to be seen as a key account of the Haitian Revolution despite the decline in popularity of James's Marxist politics. Further, the unfolding history of Haiti, much of it tragic, has done little to change the story of the country's creation.

Written in 1938, the events of the mid-twentieth century seemed to confirm James's story of revolution. Specifically, by the time the 1963 edition of the book was published, uprisings and revolutions had brought about the end of colonial rule in many countries around the world, including Kenya, India, Ghana, and Cuba. James viewed these uprisings, particularly the African ones, as coming out of the same revolutionary fabric as that of the West

Indies. This connects the events described in *The Black Jacobins* to the greater struggle for African independence and salvation. As James writes, "salvation for the West Indies lies in Africa, the original home and ancestry of the West Indian people."[1]

Limitations

The Black Jacobins is a fully West Indian book, both in setting and in style, and James does not shy away from this. In fact, he celebrates the book's cultural distinctiveness. James himself lived in several countries, however, and wrote the book while living in England. As a consequence, its cultural outlook is well rounded and includes points of view from Europe and the Americas in addition to the West Indies. Nonetheless, when James discusses the birth of a West Indian identity, for example in the book's appendix, his identification with the West Indian community and the larger African diaspora* (the dispersal of people of African origin around the world) is clear.

The book might also be limited by its political perspective. James's view of revolution and history was unashamedly Marxist. Commentators have repeatedly pointed this out, sometimes challenging James's historical credibility. One reviewer of the book describes James's relationship to Marxism: "He was a lifelong Marxist, yet one with an uncommonly fierce independence of mind that expressed itself both in his rejection of conventional Marxist arguments and in his refusal to repent of his politics even when it became fashionable to do so."[2]

This is a useful guide for thinking about how James's Marxism impacts the book; while the influence of Marxist thought is apparent throughout, the author's voice remains independent.

NOTES

1   C. L. R. James, *The Black Jacobins: Toussaint L'Ouverture and the San Domingo Revolution* (New York: Vintage Books, 1989), 399.

2   Kenan Malik, "C. L. R. James: *The Black Jacobins*," August 17, 2010, accessed November 13, 2015, http://www.kenanmalik.com/reviews/james_jacobins.html.

MODULE 8
PLACE IN THE AUTHOR'S WORK

KEY POINTS

- *The Black Jacobins* is the work of a mature, but still young, thinker.

- Marxist* ideology plays a role in the book, though to a lesser degree than elsewhere in James's overall work.

- *The Black Jacobins* is James's most significant book, and the one for which he is mostly likely to be remembered.

Positioning

C. L. R. James wrote *The Black Jacobins: Toussaint L'Ouverture and the San Domingo Revolution* when he was in his late thirties. By that time, he had already worked for several years as a journalist, and had published several books, including a notable history of communism, *World Revolution 1917–1936*, published in 1937, and *The Case for West-Indian Self-Government*, published in 1933. In 1934, four years before the publication of *The Black Jacobins*, James wrote a play based on the events in San Domingo* entitled *Toussaint L'Ouverture:* The Story of the Only Successful Slave Revolt in History*. The play was performed in 1936 at the Westminster Theatre in London with the American singer and actor Paul Robeson* as its lead. *The Black Jacobins* was, then, the product of a mature, though still relatively young, writer with a strong interest in and knowledge of the revolution in Haiti.*

Interestingly, in a 1980 interview James notes that he rewrote the play version of Toussaint O'Ouverture's story in 1967, but not the book, which "is as it always has been."[1] James suggests he would not have been able to write the book without traveling to Europe to work

> 66 If *Beyond a Boundary* is C. L. R. James's classic cultural study, *Notes on Dialectics* his crowning philosophical work, then *The Black Jacobins* is unquestionably his most important historical effort, and, arguably, the single most important historical study by any writer in the Anglophone Caribbean. 99
>
> Brian Meeks,* "Re-Reading *The Black Jacobins*: James, the Dialectic and the Revolutionary Conjuncture"

in the French National Archives. In particular, in those archives James "saw the revolution of the colonial* and underdeveloped peoples."[2]

Integration

In examining James's creative output over the course of his lifetime, strong and unifying themes emerge. One theme is of course his Marxist views. James was interested not only in the theory of Marxism, but also in understanding the communist* movement itself. James's output on Marxism is strikingly varied, including, for example, a series of essays entitled *Notes on Dialectics*, a pure discussion of Marxist philosophy built on the logic of the early eighteenth-century German philosopher G. W. F. Hegel.*

Elsewhere, James's Marxism merely plays a background role to his literary or historical goals. In *The Black Jacobins*, his political philosophy is clear in the subject matter and the book's implied call to action against imperialism* (the policy and practice adopted by a nation when it pursues political, military, and economic domination of other countries). In his memoir about cricket,* *Beyond a Boundary*, published in 1963, the themes that occupy most of James's work—colonialism, identity, class, culture, and nationalism (in the sense of a nation's pride in its own unique character and its desire to be independent of other nations)—are all seen through the prism of sport.

James's output as a writer cannot be fully understood without noting his West Indian* heritage, and his seeming interest in connecting West Indian culture to European culture. *The Black Jacobins*, which tells parallel stories of revolution (in Haiti and France), is a clear example of this, as is *Beyond a Boundary*.

Significance

The Black Jacobins is James's most recognized work. One reviewer calls it his "masterpiece."[3] It is perhaps the most likely of James's works to remain popular with future generations due to the subject matter and its wide appeal. Still, the author's body of work is so extensive that it cannot be defined just by this book. James's legacy will be different for different audiences. Marxists may be most interested in his early theoretical work; in the West Indies he is associated with his lifelong efforts to define and express the spirit of the West Indian people.

Following the publication of *The Black Jacobins* in 1938, James continued to be involved in the study of members of the African diaspora* and in their struggles. Even *Beyond a Boundary*, conceived of as a study of cricket, is seen in this light: "*Beyond a Boundary* was neither a cricket book nor an autobiography—[yet it] symbolized a new and expanded conception of humanity as the black and formerly colonial peoples burst onto the stage of world history."[4] Even in his later years, James continued to lecture and teach on similar topics, always remaining engaged with the progress of the populations of the African diaspora.

NOTES

1   C. L. R. James, "Interviews with Ken Ramchand, OWTU Guest House, San Fernando, Trinidad & Tobago," *Marxists*, September 5, 1980, accessed November 13, 2015, https://www.marxists.org/archive/james-clr/works/1980/09/banyan.htm.

2   James, "Interviews with Ken Ramchand."

3   Kenan Malik, "C. L. R. James: The Black Jacobins," August 17, 2010, *Kenan Malik*, accessed November 13, 2015, http://www.kenanmalik.com/reviews/james_jacobins.html.

4   Anna Grimshaw, "C. L. R. James: A Revolutionary Vision for the 20th Century," *Marxists*, October 8, 2000, accessed November 13, 2015, https://www.marxists.org/archive/james-clr/biograph.htm.

SECTION 3
IMPACT

THE FIRST RESPONSES

KEY POINTS

- While early reactions to the book were positive, some challenged James on ideological or technical grounds.

- James stood by the book throughout his life, making minimal changes in later editions.

- Over time, James attempted to incorporate the history of Haiti into a larger history of the West Indies* and black revolution in general.

Criticism

Initial responses to C. L. R. James's *The Black Jacobins: Toussaint L'Ouverture and the San Domingo Revolution* were largely positive, though some reviewers criticized the book for presenting a one-sided version of history. Writing in the *New Statesman*,* a notable left-of-centre publication in Britain, the journalist Flora Grierson challenged the quality of James's writing: "Careful and well documented as this history is, one's faith in Mr. James's intelligence and acumen [insight] is badly shaken by sentences such as this: 'the science of history is not what it is today and no man living could foresee, as we can foresee today, the coming upheavals.'"[1] Grierson also went on to say, "Because [James] is a Communist,* he wants to show us the worst … The intelligent historian should at least aim at impartiality," while "the fanatic cannot."[2]

The historian Rayford Logan* largely embraced the book for providing a description of the slave* revolt with "infinitely more historical accuracy" than previous writers, but he challenged James on several points.[3] One is technical: Logan suggested James could have

> ❝ *The Black Jacobins* is not academic history, but one written by a proletarian revolutionist using theory and history as a guide to revolutionary struggle. ❞
>
> Ashley Smith,* *International Socialist Review*

made better use of primary sources and could have discussed further the role of the "diplomacy of the United States and of Great Britain." A second criticism is stylistic, as Logan questions the "applicability of the term 'Jacobins'* to the slaves of Saint-Domingue [San Domingo*]."[4]

Much of the early positive reaction to the book focused on the style of James's writing and his approach to history. One scholar called the book a "brilliantly written and conceived history," and agreed with James's argument that the revolution in Haiti* was part of the larger French Revolution.*[5]

Responses

James did not respond directly to criticisms that his version of history was too political. In fact, in the preface to the 1962 edition, James writes, "Today, I have little to add to or subtract from the fundamental ideas" in the original publication. He goes on to say, "Where they [the fundamental ideas in *The Black Jacobins*] fly in the face of historical events I have omitted or altered them [the historical events in Haiti], never more than to the extent of a few lines."[6] James does note in the same text that his intention in the final pages of the book was to "stimulate the coming emancipation of Africa," an admission that partly makes the book different from purely academic, and neutral, history.[7]

One significant addition to the book in later editions is the appendix "From Toussaint L'Ouverture* to Fidel Castro,"* which first appeared in the 1963 edition. The appendix attempts to position the

Haitian Revolution, led by L'Ouverture, and the revolution in Cuba,* led by the Cuban revolutionary Fidel Castro, in the context of West Indian history. James links the two events as follows: "West Indians first became aware of themselves as a people in the Haitian Revolution. Whatever its ultimate fate, the Cuban Revolution marks the ultimate stage of a Caribbean quest for national identity."[8]

Conflict and Consensus

Though the book's main themes were not changed by James in subsequent editions, the author did revisit the text from time to time throughout his life with a new viewpoint. In 1971, for example, he imagined a world of increasing revolution—this was after the decline of colonial* rule around the world—and suggested that a revised edition of the book would focus on the psychologies of the slaves of the island. In particular, it would connect "the actual statements of the slaves telling what they were doing" with similar statements in France, where revolution was unfolding as well.[9]

Indeed, as colonial rule dissolved in the mid-twentieth century, the context in which *The Black Jacobins* was viewed changed as well. While at the time of the book's publication in 1938, the Haitian Revolution was presented as a remarkable and unlikely event, by the 1960s and 1970s it appeared to be connected to a longer tradition of revolution. Further, while in James's first edition Toussaint L'Ouverture is presented as a notable and unique character, James's later writing seems to place L'Ouverture in the context of the independence struggles of other former colonies during the twentieth century, mainly in Africa and Asia. In his 1962 preface to the book, James refers to his own attempt to craft the story of Haiti into a coherent history of the West Indies: "Writers on the West Indies always relate them to their approximation to Britain, France, Spain, and America, that is to say, to Western civilization, never in relation to their own history. This is here attempted for the first time."[10] In other words, James felt that the

Haitian Revolution could be seen as an early example of a long history of people in the former colonies fighting to be free.

NOTES

1   Flora Grierson, "Man's Inhumanity to Man," *New Statesman*, October 8, 1938.

2   Grierson, "Man's Inhumanity."

3   Rayford Logan in Aldon Lynn Nielsen, *C. L. R. James: A Critical Introduction* (Jackson: University Press of Mississippi, 2010), 64.

4   Nielson, *Critical Introduction*, 64.

5   Nielson, *Critical Introduction*, 64

6   C. L. R. James, *The Black Jacobins: Toussaint L'Ouverture and the San Domingo Revolution* (New York: Vintage Books, 1989), preface.

7   James, *Black Jacobins*, preface.

8   James, *Black Jacobins*, 391.

9   C. L. R. James in "C. L. R. James Revises *The Black Jacobins*," *Long Way from Home*, January 21, 2010, accessed November 13, 2015, http://fragments-correspondence.org/2010/01/clr-james-revises-the-black-jacobins/.

10 James, *Black Jacobins*, vii.

MODULE 10
THE EVOLVING DEBATE

KEY POINTS

- *The Black Jacobins* had an important impact on the debate within left- wing politics about whether industrialized countries had to make their own socialist revolutions before the poor countries could follow.

- The book helped pave the way for later works of "history from below,"* and is associated with the school of subaltern studies* that emerged well after the book's 1938 publication and that examines issues connected with "voiceless" people of low social and economic status in former colonies.

- Today, James's legacy is likely to be more felt in art and culture than in academic discourse.

Uses and Problems

C. L. R. James's *The Black Jacobins: Toussaint L'Ouverture and the San Domingo Revolution* has had a major influence on a variety of subjects since its publication. Perhaps most immediately, the book played a role in the debates within the leftist politics of the 1930s and 1940s. The book challenged two key parts of Marxist* thought at the time: first, the idea that "the revolution would take place first in Europe, in the advanced capitalist countries, and that this would act as a model and a catalyst for the later upheavals in the underdeveloped world"; and second, that to be successful, the revolution needed a core of "specially trained leaders."[1] *The Black Jacobins* challenged both these key ideas by describing a successful revolution against a European power (France) carried out by the uneducated slaves* of one of their most profitable colonies. This analysis allied James with the Trotskyist* branch of the

> **"** It is as a prose poem to 'man's unconquerable mind,' and as an unflinching portrait of the human meaning of the struggle for freedom, that we should read, and celebrate, *The Black Jacobins.* **"**
>
> Kenan Malik,* in his review of *The Black Jacobins: Toussaint L'Ouverture and the San Domingo Revolution*

revolutionary left, which proclaimed that people of the poor countries could carry out their own socialist revolutions without waiting to be led by revolutions in the industrialized countries first.

This type of historical analysis laid the groundwork for what would later become known as "history from below." One of the notable historians who developed that style was the influential British scholar E. P. Thompson.* His 1963 book *The Making of the English Working Class* "launched a current in Marxist history which restored the exploited and oppressed to their rightful place as makers of history."[2] The Canadian political scientist David McNally* observes that, prior to Thompson's book, one of the few works to explore this theme was *The Black Jacobins*, noting that such work grew out of the Trotskyist tradition of which James was a part.

Schools of Thought

The Black Jacobins has been associated at different times with several schools of thought, including postcolonial studies* and subaltern studies. Both schools emerged in the 1980s and focus on how colonialism* has affected the colonized populations (and, in the case of subaltern studies, the experiences of the poorest populations). James's influence on these disciplines has not always been recognized, and to some extent the book is an early example of a style of scholarship that was later given a name. The Australian scholar Brian

Stoddart* refers to James as an "unknown, sometimes unrecognized force" in the development of what is now considered subaltern studies.[3]

The core concept of subaltern studies is to study, and tell the story of, populations that have been excluded from traditional power structures, including the working poor and the peasants of former colonies. This discipline emerged as colonialism was ending, and has its roots in telling the colonial history from the point of view of the colonized rather than the colonizer. One of the notable scholars of the discipline, Gayatri Chakravorty Spivak,* says that subaltern is "not just a classy word for oppressed."[4] She states that the working class in the industrialized countries, while an oppressed group, is not subaltern, as it exists within the mainstream global cultural hegemony* (that is, it exists within the culture that dominates the cultural lives of the people of the poor countries). Other groups, however—like the poor and uneducated in the poor countries—are subaltern because they *have* been fully excluded.

In Current Scholarship

Few writers today embody the breadth of experiences and interests, and the passion, that characterized James's career. In fact, James's spirit is probably more alive in art than in scholarship. As a journalist, James was always more oriented towards street culture (that is, culture as practiced by ordinary people) rather than the academic world (universities, research institutes, and so on), and he recognized that the cultural outputs of African (or West Indian*) culture often existed in the oral (spoken) realm of the street. James himself made this observation in reference to American jazz and blues, writing that "the greatest artists of our day have been people who somehow have found themselves in circumstances in which they did not write or work for the educated intellectual public, as all these other writers do, but found themselves compelled to appeal to the ordinary citizen."[5]

In a sense, James is describing a key feature of popular music, much of which grew out of African art forms—that the struggle of the artist is also a universal struggle. Today, the most notable example of this process is hip-hop, an art form rooted in African experience and culture but also deeply mainstream. As an example, in 2004 the rapper Chuck D* expressed a perspective on leadership that seems to draw from James's view that oppressed people don't need to look to others to free them. Like Toussaint L'Ouverture, they can lead their own struggle for freedom: "There are too many leaders anointed because they have a public voice—television, radio, or record, or whatever. That even includes myself. In the past, I'd say, 'Don't anoint me when you can anoint yourself.'"[6]

NOTES

1   Anna Grimshaw, "C. L. R. James: A Revolutionary Vision for the 20th Century," accessed November 13, 2015, https://www.marxists.org/archive/james-clr/biograph.htm.

2   David McNally, "E. P. Thompson: Class Struggle and Historical Materialism," *International Socialism Journal* 61 (1993), accessed November 13, 2015, http://pubs.socialistreviewindex.org.uk/isj61/mcnally.htm.

3   Brian Stoddart, *Sport, Culture and History: Region, Nation and Globe* (New York: Routledge, 2013).

4   Leon de Kock, "Interview With Gayatri Chakravorty Spivak: New Nation Writers Conference in South Africa," Ariel: A Review of International English Literature, 23.3 (1992), 29-47.

5   C. L. R. James in Paul Ortiz, "C. L. R. James's Visionary Legacy," *Solidarity*, January/February 2012, accessed November 13, 2015, http://www.solidarity-us.org/site/node/3494#R3.

6   Jeff Chang, "Rapping the Vote with Chuck D," *Mother Jones*, September/October 2004, accessed November 13, 2015, http://www.motherjones.com/media/2004/09/chuck-d.

MODULE 11
IMPACT AND INFLUENCE TODAY

KEY POINTS

- In academic circles, *The Black Jacobins* remains an important work of West Indian* and African diaspora* identity; the African diaspora denotes the dispersal of black African people throughout the world.

- The themes of *The Black Jacobins* are still relevant for present-day revolutionaries, such as those involved in the uprisings that began to sweep the Arab world in 2010 known as the Arab Spring.*

- Conditions have changed, however, and today revolution takes place in a much more connected world, economically, culturally, and technologically.

Position

C. L. R. James's *The Black Jacobins: Toussaint L'Ouverture and the San Domingo Revolution* is still an important book in the history of the West Indies and in the subfields of Marxist* history and subaltern studies.* It is widely considered to be a classic. In the West Indies, the book is very highly regarded and remains a topic of academic conversation. As such, the book's importance extends beyond its accurate portrayal of events, and serves as a centerpiece for a tradition of radical scholarship in the region. Graciela Chailloux Laffita,* a professor of economics at the University of Havana, describes the book in the following terms: "*The Black Jacobins* is, above all, a weapon in the struggle against colonialism,* racism, and imperialism,* a work that looks to the future."[1]

Outside of this tradition, the book is still widely read on college campuses around the world. For example, in a course at New York

> ❝ The headline-grabbing revolutions that gripped the Middle East in early 2011 brought the promise of an "Arab Spring," a new dawn for democracy in a region with a history of autocracy. But the real result, as it turned out, was in many cases almost the opposite: a wave of violence, repression and civil war. ❞
>
> Carol J. Williams,* "Where the Arab Spring Revolutions Went Wrong"

University entitled "Concepts in Postcolonial Theory: The Subaltern; and the Postcolonial Intellectual," *The Black Jacobins* is assigned as an example of "history from below."*[2] In a course at the University of Virginia, entitled "Cross-Currents in the African Diaspora," James's appendix to his book is assigned as an example of intellectual trends in the African diaspora.[3] Interestingly, *The Black Jacobins* is used as a book about African and West Indian identity as much as it is about revolution in Marxist theory.

Interaction

While discussion of *The Black Jacobins* is today largely limited to academic circles (with a few notable exceptions), discussions about political and social revolution are not. The uprisings known as the Arab Spring are a notable example. Using communication technologies* such as Facebook and Twitter to spread their message, citizens of Egypt, Tunisia, Libya, Yemen, and elsewhere in the region united under the chant, "The people want to topple the regime."[4] To date, these revolutions have mostly had the effect of destabilizing the Middle Eastern region politically and their ultimate outcome is unknown.

It would be a mistake to draw a direct line between the revolt in Haiti* and today's revolutions, or even between James's Marxist interpretation of revolution and current events. In many ways, the Arab Spring represents a new kind of revolution. Referencing certain political institutions that sought to further revolutionary ends, the American scholar of international relations. William Zartman* writes, "In classical revolutionary terms, in the Arab Spring uprisings there is no [National] Convention and no Jacobin Club* as in France, no Communist Party as in Russia, no mullah* network as in Iran, and were there one it would be deconstructed by the social media."[5] It is too early to diagnose the current state of revolution in ideological terms, though it seems likely that an ideological theme will emerge.

The Continuing Debate

Despite the revolutionary energy of the present moment, in the Arab world and elsewhere, economic and cultural conditions complicate the outlook for revolution. In an opinion column for the *New York Times* titled "The Limits of 21st-Century Revolution," the writer Roger Cohen* lists eight factors of twenty-first century politics that complicate modern revolutionary movements. Specifically, the essay considers the limitations to former President Hugo Chávez's* attempt to carry out revolutionary socialist reform in Venezuela. The first observation on Cohen's list—"trade trumps politics"—may be most important.[6] Since the 1980s, global markets have become much more integrated, making most countries of the world economic partners in some way. For example, while in the mid-2000s the United States and Venezuela were political enemies, they were also economic partners: "Even as [the Venezuelan leader Hugo] Chávez* has been calling President [George W.] Bush* 'the devil,' US–Venezuela commercial ties have blossomed. This is the Western hemisphere's equivalent of the Taiwan–China relationship:* political enemies engaged in booming business."[7]

The last of Cohen's observations is also important—"TV trumps all"—although today "the Internet trumps all" is more appropriate. As

Cohen writes, "In the bars of Caracas, people watch NBA basketball and their beloved baseball."[8] While it could be argued that the Haitian Revolution would not have occurred without the exchange of information between France and San Domingo,* it is worth considering whether the rapid pace of communication and the intermingling of cultures around the world has made major political upheaval less—or more—likely.

NOTES

1   Graciela Chailloux Laffita, "The Black Jacobins: Teachers of Revolution," *Caminos* 48 (2008), accessed November 13, 2015, http://www. normangirvan.info/wp-content/uploads/2009/03/the-black-jacobins-graciela- challoux2.pdf.

2   Rajeswari Sunder Rajan, "Concepts in Postcolonial Theory: The Subaltern; and the Postcolonial Intellectual," New York University, accessed November 13, 2015, http://english.fas.nyu.edu/docs/IO/7316/G41.2900(001) SunderRajanSyllabus.pdf.

3   Corey Walker, "Cross-currents in the African Diaspora," University of Virginia, 2004, accessed November 13, 2015, http://www.virginia.edu/woodson/ courses/aas102/syllabus2004.html.

4   Fouad Ajami, "The Arab Spring at One," *Foreign Affairs* (March/April 2012), accessed November 13, 2015, https://www.foreignaffairs.com/articles/ syria/2012-01-24/arab-spring-one.

5   I. William Zartman, ed., *Arab Spring: Negotiating in the Shadow of the Intifadat* (Athens: University of Georgia Press, 2015), 20–1.

6   Roger Cohen, "The Limits of 21st-Century Revolution," *New York Times*, December 3, 2007, accessed January 21, 2016, www.nytimes. com/2007/12/03/opinion/03cohen.html.

7   Cohen, "Limits."

8   Cohen, "Limits."

WHERE NEXT?

KEY POINTS

- *The Black Jacobins* will likely continue to be a definitive account of the Haitian Revolution.*

- Much of the contemporary discussion of the Haitian Revolution occurs in popular culture, for example by the actor Danny Glover* and the Haitian musician Wyclef Jean.*

- Students will benefit from *The Black Jacobins* as history, and as a challenge to the ideas they already have about the world.

Potential

C. L. R. James's *The Black Jacobins: Toussaint L'Ouverture and the San Domingo Revolution* will almost certainly retain its position as a definitive history of the Haitian Revolution. The emotional power of the book, however, will likely be especially felt by audiences with some connection, either by history or circumstance, to the struggle that the revolution represents. One of those audiences is African Americans. Following the earthquake in Haiti in 2010, a correspondent for CNN, Peniel E. Joseph,* wrote, "For African Americans, Haiti's tragedy hits close to home. For more than two centuries the tiny, at times fragile, republic has inspired black political activism in the United States."[1] It is important to note that the Haitian Revolution took place more than 50 years before slavery* was finally outlawed in the United States, and throughout the course of the African American struggle for civil rights, Joseph states, "Haiti profoundly impacted the imagination of African American political activism."[2]

> ❝ Haiti is just a fulcrum for everything horrible and good. It has this intense magical belief that is pretty amazing. And it's been the subject of exploitation and violence since the beginning. But it was also the site of the first successful slave revolt. ❞
>
> Michael Gira,* quoted in "Q&A: Michael Gira of Swans on *To Be Kind, Proper Crowdfunding, and the Human Voice*"

The civil rights struggle continues in the United States and elsewhere, and Haiti's example remains an important part of its history. No book represents that history more clearly and passionately than *The Black Jacobins*. As Joseph recalls in his article connecting the two traditions, "C. L. R. James, a Trinidadian-born author and activist, wrote a 1939 [sic] history of the revolt, *The Black Jacobins*, that remains a classic in Africana studies scholarship."[3]

Future Directions

The character of Toussaint L'Ouverture* is still reflected in popular culture, and several modern-day artists have carried out projects inspired by his revolution. The future relevance of the story of revolution is most likely to live in these artistic works. As an example, the Haitian rapper Wyclef Jean released an album in 2009 entitled *From the Hut, to the Projects, to the Mansion*, in which Jean adopts the persona of a character based on L'Ouverture.[4] The themes of the album include Jean's seeming exclusion from the rap community and document his reemergence in revolutionary terms. Jean's message for the record mirrors L'Ouverture's unlikely triumph: "The point is, whatever you want to do, you can accomplish. If I came from nothing and became something, if I was chosen for greatness, then so can you."[5]

As another example, in 2006 the American actor Danny Glover founded Louverture Films, a production company dedicated to making films of "historical relevance, social purpose, commercial value, and artistic integrity."[6] The company's name is the result of Glover's strong connection to the revolution in Haiti. Noting that he discovered the story of L'Ouverture after reading *The Black Jacobins*, Glover told the *Guardian* newspaper in 2012, "When I talk about Haiti, it breaks my heart … Yet when I think about the Haitian people's resilience, it heals my heart at the same time … And since the moment they organized that revolution, they have been defeated on, they've been undermined, yet they keep organizing."[7]

Summary

The Black Jacobins is a groundbreaking work in the history of the West Indies* and political revolutions in general. As a work of history, it draws in readers on many levels. It is passionately written and filled with historical detail. It is politically daring—James does not hesitate to inject the story with emotion, observation, and ideology. Moreover, it uniquely tells an important story from the bottom up, and in so doing was a pathbreaking work in historical studies. Despite the book's politicized nature, it is considered today to be an accurate account. One contemporary reviewer notes, "Over the course of the text, L'Ouverture comes to act almost as a tragic hero, and this is where the fine line between accurate history and historical literature is blurred, because although *The Black Jacobins* is probably the best account of the revolution that exists, it can seem idealistic at times. This idealism might be one reason it has become such an influential book. It has become a touchstone for thinking about the decolonization* struggle."[8]

Students reading the book will benefit most if they ask themselves to consider whether the story of the Haitian Revolution overturns their ideas about the economic trajectories of all nations. As Glover's quote above indicates, the nation of Haiti has continued to struggle immensely since its establishment in 1804. It is important for readers to consider the circumstances of the present in relation to the past, and to look for opportunities to think about how "history from below"* might change the mainstream explanation of events.

NOTES

1   Peniel E. Joseph, "Haiti's revolt inspired US black activists," CNN, January 27, 2010, accessed November 13, 2015, http:/www.cnn.com/2010/OPINION/01/26/joseph.african.americans.haiti/.

2   Joseph, "Haiti's revolt."

3   Joseph, "Haiti's revolt."

4   Mariel Concepcion, "Wyclef Revisits Hip-Hop Roots On 'Toussaint: St. Jean' EP," *Billboard*, November 20, 2009, accessed November 14, 2015, http://www.billboard.com/articles/news/266628/wyclef-revisits-hip-hop-roots-on-toussaint-st-jean-ep.

5   Concepcion, "Wyclef Revisits."

6   Sasha Panaram, "Toussaint: The Heartbeat of Freedom," *Black Atlantic*, March 6, 2014, accessed November 14, 2015, http:/sites.duke.edu/blackatlantic/2014/03/06/toussaint-the-heartbeat-of-freedom/#_ftn1.

7   Stuart Jeffries, "Danny Glover: the Good Cop," *Guardian*, May 18, 2012, accessed November 14, 2015, http:/www.theguardian.com/film/2012/may/18/danny-glover-good-cop.

8   Western Michigan University, "The Black Jacobins," *Colonial & Postcolonial Literary Dialogues*, April 16, 2001, accessed November 13, 2015, http://wmich.edu/dialogues/texts/blackjacobins.html.

GLOSSARY

GLOSSARY OF TERMS

American Revolution: a period of political upheaval between 1775 and 1783 when colonists from thirteen of Britain's colonies in North America challenged the British monarchy, resulting in the founding of the United States of America.

Arab Spring: a series of protests and political revolutions, starting in late 2010, in several countries in the Middle East and North Africa. The protests, in which social media played an important role, were largely provoked by a desire for democratic government.

Bourgeoisie: a Marxist term referring to the social class that owns the majority of resources in a capitalist society.

Capitalism: an economic system in which transactions take place in markets between willing buyers and willing sellers for the sake of private profit. Capitalists are those who own economic resources and can earn money by investing those resources in economic activities with the aim of making a profit.

Colonialism: political control by one country of another territory and its inhabitants, usually by occupying the territory with settlers and exploiting its resources.

Communism: an ideology developed by Karl Marx and Friedrich Engels that advocates the common ownership of the means of production (the resources required for producing goods) along with the abolition of social classes.

Cricket: a game, very roughly similar to baseball, in which two teams of 11 players use a bat and ball to score.

Cuban Revolution: a political revolt that took place from 1953 to 1959 that overthrew the Cuban president and established the island as a socialist state. Its primary leader was Fidel Castro.

Cultural hegemony: a theory developed by the Italian Marxist thinker Antonio Gramsci stating that dominant social classes control not only the economy, but also the culture of a society.

Dialectic: in this case, a philosophical concept presented by the German philosopher Georg Hegel in which the tension created between an idea or concept and the reaction that rises up in opposition to it (the antithesis) leads to a synthesis—a resolution. Karl Marx built on this idea to develop his notion of historical materialism.

Diaspora: a word describing ethnic populations who have migrated to a different place away from their homeland.

Enlightenment: a philosophical movement in the eighteenth century based on the principles of liberty, reason, and tolerance. The Enlightenment saw some of the earliest efforts to apply scientific principles to social life.

Fascism: a radical right-wing form of government characterized by totalitarianism (the intrusion of government into every area of life), strong nationalism, and economic isolation.

French Revolution: a period of sociopolitical turmoil in France from 1789 to 1799 that resulted in the abolition of the French monarchy.

Great Depression: a global economic crisis that began with the American stock market crash of 1929 and lasted until the onset of

World War II. It led to major changes in international economic policy.

Haitian Revolution: the first and only successful slave revolt, which took place between 1791 and 1803. Its result was the establishment of the Republic of Haiti in 1804.

Historical materialism: an approach developed by the political philosopher Karl Marx, according to which history is driven by economic forces, or tensions in the way the means of production (the resources required for producing goods) are owned and organized in society.

History from below: the study of history from the viewpoint of marginalized groups, including the economically or socially oppressed.

Imperialism: a foreign policy in which a nation extends its influence beyond its borders to dominate other countries, using military, cultural, or economic force.

Jacobins: the members of the Jacobin Club (who were known as Jacobins) were the most radical and ruthless supporters of the French Revolution. At its height, the club, which was founded on October 6, 1789, had a membership of half a million.

Marxism: a school of philosophy inspired by the work of Karl Marx. Some of its core features are historical materialism and a class-based method of social analysis.

McCarthyism: a political movement in the United States in the 1950s, led by US senator Joseph McCarthy, that aimed to rid the civil and military establishment and entertainment industry of communists.

Means of production: a Marxist term describing all the physical inputs (natural resources like wool or steel) and tools (like plows, machines, and computers) that humans use to produce goods and services. Communists advocate transferring ownership of the means of production from individuals to society in general.

Monarchy: a form of governance in which power is centralized under a hereditary king or queen.

Mulatto: a term, now generally considered derogatory, to describe a person of mixed white and black heritage.

Mullah: a member of a network of religious figures with political influence in Iran.

New Statesman: a British magazine founded in 1913 by members of the Fabian Society, a left-of-center socialist organization. It continues to be published today.

Olympic Games: international sporting games and competitions where athletes from over 200 nations around the world compete every four years. The games are based on competitions in ancient Greece.

Pan-Africanism: a movement based on the idea that unity among Africans worldwide is critical to progress at all levels—social, economic, and political.

Postcolonialism: the academic field that studies the various economic, linguistic, and cultural legacies of the colonial period.

Proletariat: a Marxist word to describe the working class in a capitalist society.

Russian Revolution: the name used for the two revolutions that occurred in Russia in 1917, leading to the collapse of Tsarist rule and the eventual establishment of the Soviet Union in 1922 after a period of civil war. The first, in March, led to the resignation of Nicolas II; in the second, in October, the communist Bolsheviks, led by Vladimir Lenin, overthrew the Provisional Government to take power.

San Domingo: the colonial name for present-day Haiti.

Slavery: a set of laws that extend property rights to the ownership of human beings. Slavery was the foundation of the economy in San Domingo, and throughout the West Indies, by the mid-eighteenth century. France abolished slavery in 1794, though briefly reinstated the institution in San Domingo in 1802 before its final abolition in 1804. Following abolition in present-day Haiti, slavery flourished in Cuba where it was eventually abolished in 1886.

Social media: a set of technological tools that enable rapid and mass global communication over the Internet.

Soviet Union: the Union of Soviet Socialist Republics (USSR) was a Eurasian empire that arose from the Russian Revolution in 1917, and consisted of Russia and 14 satellite states in Eastern Europe, the Baltic and Black Seas, and Central Asia. It existed from 1922 to 1991.

Stalinism: the set of policies and views related to Joseph Stalin's leadership of the Soviet Union from the mid-1920s until his death in 1953. A key component was the idea of "socialism in one country," which held that the socialist movement should first consolidate in Russia before expanding, rather than carry out simultaneous global revolution.

Subaltern studies: an academic discipline that grew out of an international network of scholars known as the Subaltern Studies Group, largely composed of South Asian scholars, and concerned with postcolonial societies. The term "subaltern" refers to a person or group of inferior rank (as defined by the dominant group) whether in reference to race, ethnicity, class, gender, religion, or sexual orientation.

Taiwan–China relationship: there has been a tense political relationship between the two countries since 1949 which saw the establishment of a communist government in China, and a nationalist government opposed to communist rule in Taiwan. Despite political tensions, both countries engage in significant trade with each other.

Trotskyism: the political ideology set out by the Russian revolutionary Leon Trotsky that advocated permanent revolution— a worldwide revolution of the working class against capitalists.

West Indies: the islands of the Caribbean Sea including, among other nations, Cuba, Haiti, Jamaica, and the Bahamas; some definitions include several coastal countries, including Guyana.

World War I: a military conflict between 1914 and 1918 that involved all of the world's key powers, including the United States, France, Italy, Britain, Germany, Russia and Austria-Hungary.

World War II: a global war from 1939 to 1945 centered primarily in Europe and Japan that dramatically changed the dynamic of world power. The war was finally provoked by the German leader Adolf Hitler's attempts to expand German territories.

PEOPLE MENTIONED IN THE TEXT

Napoleon Bonaparte (1769–1821) was emperor of France from 1804 to 1814. He rose to prominence as a military leader in the French Revolution.

George W. Bush (b. 1946) is an American who served as the 43rd president of the United States. His presidency was controversial largely due to the military invasion of Iraq that began in 2003.

Fidel Castro (b. 1926) was the leader of the Cuban Revolution and the President of Cuba 1976–2008.

Dipesh Chakrabarty (b. 1948) is an Indian historian who currently teaches at the University of Chicago. He is known for his contributions to subaltern studies.

Hugo Chávez (1954–2013) was a Venezuelan politician who served as president of Venezuela from 1999 to his death in 2013. He was known for his efforts to carry out a socialist transformation of Venezuelan society.

Chuck D (b. 1960) is the stage name of an American musician best known as leader of the hip-hop group Public Enemy.

Roger Cohen (b. 1955) is a London-born writer who contributes to the *New York Times*. He has often written in favor of a strong American presence in international affairs.

Jean-Jacques Dessalines (1758–1806) was a leader of the Haitian Revolution and the first emperor of Haiti. Dessalines became leader of the revolution after Toussaint L'Ouverture was captured in 1802.

Friedrich Engels (1820–95) was a German philosopher who developed the core principles of Marxist theory along with Karl Marx. Engels coauthored *The Communist Manifesto* (1848) with Marx.

Francisco Franco (1892–1975) was the extreme right-wing leader of Spain from 1936 to his death in 1975.

Marcus Garvey (1887–1940) was a native of Jamaica and activist representing black nationalism and pan-Africanism. He founded a number of organizations including the Universal Negro Improvement Association and African Communities League (known as UNIA-ACL), and the Black Star Line, a shipping company.

Michael Gira (b. 1954) is an American musician known for his work with the groups Swans and Angels of Light.

Danny Glover (b. 1946) is an American actor best known for his role in the *Lethal Weapon* movies.

Antonio Gramsci (1891–1937) was an Italian Marxist, theorist, and politician best known for his *Prison Notebooks*, which introduced the notion of cultural hegemony. He founded the Communist Party in Italy.

Georg Wilhelm Friedrich Hegel (1770–1831) was a German philosopher interested in political philosophy, the philosophy of history, logic, and aesthetics. Hegel is perhaps best known for one of the four works he produced in his lifetime, *The Phenomenology of Spirit* (1807).

Robert Hill (b. 1943) is a Jamaican-born historian who has spent much of his career at UCLA (University of California, Los Angeles).

Wyclef Jean (b. 1969) is a Haitian musician best known for his involvement in the popular hip-hop group the Fugees. In 2010, he attempted to run for president of Haiti but did not meet the residency requirement.

Thomas Jefferson (1743–1826) was the third president of the United States and principal author of the Declaration of Independence. His presidency was notable for the Louisiana Purchase (the purchase of territory from France in 1803), which greatly increased the size of the United States.

Peniel E. Joseph (b. 1973) is an American historian currently serving as professor of public affairs at the University of Texas, Austin. Prior to this appointment he founded the Center for the Study of Race and Democracy at Tufts University in Medford, Massachusetts. Joseph studies the black power movement.

Graciela Chailloux Laffita is a Cuban scholar affiliated to the University of Havana and the Center for the Study of the United States in Havana.

Charles Leclerc (1772–1802) was a French military general who led an expedition to San Domingo to reinstate slavery in 1801. Leclerc was married to Napoleon Bonaparte's sister, Pauline.

Vladmir Lenin (1870–1924) was a Russian revolutionary and political theorist known for his leadership during the Russian Revolution. He served as leader of the Soviet Union from 1922 to 1924.

Rayford Logan (1897–1982) was a professor at Howard University, Washington, DC, a pan-African activist and African American historian known for his contributions to the study of post-

Reconstruction Era America (that is, the period after the American Civil War, 1865–77). Logan was an advisor to the National Association for the Advancement of Colored People (NAACP) in the 1940s.

Toussaint L'Ouverture (1743–1803) was a former slave who led the slave revolt of San Domingo to freedom. L'Ouverture established himself as dictator of the whole island in 1801, but was deposed and eventually killed in 1803 prior to the establishment of Haiti.

Kenan Malik (b. 1960) is an English writer who covers a variety of subjects, including biology, culture, race, and politics, and is known for his 1996 book *The Meaning of Race*.

Karl Marx (1818–83) was an economist, philosopher, writer, and revolutionary best known for *The Communist Manifesto* (1848), coauthored with Engels, and *Das Kapital* (1867–94). He helped develop the political principles of communism.

Joseph McCarthy (1908–57) was an American politician who served as a Republican senator from Wisconsin from 1947 to 1957. He is best known for his efforts to identify and undermine what he saw as communist activity in the US government.

David McNally is a Canadian political scientist who currently teaches at York University in Toronto. He primarily writes on socialist politics.

Brian Meeks (b. 1953) is a Canadian-born Jamaican writer whose writing covers the radical politics of the Caribbean.

Kwame Nkrumah (1909–72) was a Ghanaian politician who served as the first president of Ghana from 1960 to 1966 after leading the country in its effort to end British colonial rule.

Thomas Paine (1737–1809) was an English American revolutionary, philosopher, writer, and political activist, and one of America's Founding Fathers (meaning the key individuals who led the American Revolution against Britain).

Pericles (495–429 B.C.E.) was arguably the most influential statesman and orator of Athenian society between the Persian and Peloponnesian wars.

Paul Robeson (1898–1976) was an African American actor and activist, whose criticism of the United States government led to him being blacklisted during the McCarthy era.

Ashley Smith is an American writer who covers socialist politics and is a member of the editorial board of the *International Socialist Review*.

Gayatri Chakravorty Spivak (b. 1942) is an Indian philosopher known for her contributions to postcolonialism, most notably her essay, "Can the Subaltern Speak?" She is currently university professor at Columbia University, New York.

Joseph Stalin (1878–1953) was the dictator of the Soviet Union until 1953. After becoming General Secretary of the Central Committee of the Communist Party in 1922, he began ruthlessly eliminating all opposition to his rule.

Brian Stoddart is an Australian scholar who has written on the intermingling of history and sports.

E. P. Thompson (1924–93) was a British historian best known for his work *The Making of the English Working* Class, published in 1963 and considered an example of "history from below." Thompson was a Marxist.

Leon Trotsky (1879–1940) was a Marxist theorist and revolutionary who was the founding leader of the Red Army that defeated the forces opposed to the Bolsheviks during Russia's civil war, thereby consolidating the communists' hold on power. He was intellectually opposed to Stalin.

Carol J. Williams is an American journalist who writes on international affairs for the *Los Angeles Times*.

I. William Zartman (b. 1932) is an American scholar of international relations who is currently professor emeritus at the Paul H. Nitze School of Advanced International Studies at Johns Hopkins University.

WORKS CITED

WORKS CITED

Ajami, Fouad. "The Arab Spring at One." *Foreign Affairs* (March/April 2012). Accessed November 13, 2015. https://www.foreignaffairs.com/articles/syria/2012-01–24/arab-spring-one.

Chakrabarty, Dipesh. "Subaltern Studies and Postcolonial Historiography." *Nepantla: Views from South* 1, no. 1 (2000): 14.

Chang, Jeff. "Rapping the Vote with Chuck D." *Mother Jones* (September/October 2004). Accessed November 13, 2015. http://www.motherjones.com/media/2004/09/chuck-d.

Cohen, Roger. "The Limits of 21st-Century Revolution." *New York Times*, December 3, 2007. Accessed January 21, 2016. www.nytimes.com/2007/12/03/opinion/03cohen.html.

Concepcion, Mariel. "Wyclef Revisits Hip-Hop Roots On 'Toussaint: St. Jean' EP." *Billboard*, November 20, 2009. Accessed November 14, 2015. http://www.billboard.com/articles/news/266628/wyclef-revisits-hip-hop-roots-on-toussaint-st-jean-ep.

de Kock, Leon. "Interview With Gayatri Chakravorty Spivak: New Nation Writers Conference in South Africa." Northern Arizona University, December 1991. Accessed November 13, 2015. http://jan.ucc.nau.edu/~sj6/Spivak%20Interview%20DeKock.pdf.

Fraser, C. Gerald. "C. L. R. James, Historian, Critic and Pan-Africanist, is Dead at 88." *New York Times*, June 2, 1989. Accessed January 21, 2016. http://www.nytimes.com/1989/06/02/obituaries/c-l-r-james-historian-critic-and-pan-africanist-is-dead-at-88.html?_r=0.

Gramsci, Antonio. *Selections from the Prison Notebooks.* New York: International Publishers, 1971.

Grierson, Flora. "Man's Inhumanity to Man." *New Statesman*, October 8, 1938.

Grimshaw, Anna. "C. L. R. James: A Revolutionary Vision for the 20th Century." *Marxists*, October 8, 2000. Accessed November 13, 2015. https://www.marxists.org/archive/james-clr/biograph.htm.

Hill, Robert A. "In England, 1932–38." In *C. L. R. James: His Life and Work*, edited by Paul Buhle. London: Allison and Busby, 1986.

James, C. L. R. "Interviews with Ken Ramchand, OWTU Guest House, San Fernando, Trinidad & Tobago." *Marxists*, September 5, 1980. Accessed November 13, 2015. https://www.marxists.org/archive/james-clr/works/1980/09/banyan.htm.

Notes on Dialectics: Hegel, Marx, Lenin. London: Allison and Busby, 1980.

The Black Jacobins: Toussaint L'Ouverture and the San Domingo Revolution. New York: Vintage Books, 1989.

Beyond a Boundary. Durham, NC: Duke University Press, 1993.

Beyond a Boundary. Durham, NC: Duke University Press, 1993.

World Revolution 1917–1936. Amherst, NY: Humanity Books, 1993.

"C. L. R. James Revises *The Black Jacobins*." *Long Way from Home*, January 21, 2010. Accessed November 13, 2015. http://fragments-correspondence. org/2010/01/clr-james-revises-the-black-jacobins/.

Toussaint L'Ouverture: The Story of the Only Successful Slave Revolt in History: A Play in Three Acts. Durham, NC: Duke University Press, 2012.

The Life of Captain Cipriani: An Account of British Government in the West Indies, with the Pamphlet The Case for West Indian Self-Government. Durham, NC: Duke University Press, 2014.

"After Hitler, Our Turn." In *World Revolution 1917–1936*. *Marxists*. Accessed November 13, 2015. https://www.marxists.org/archive/james-clr/works/world/ ch12.htm.

Papers, boxes 2 and 5, Rare Book & Manuscript Library, Columbia University Library, New York.

Jeffries, Stuart. "Danny Glover: The Good Cop." *Guardian*, May 18, 2012. Accessed November 14, 2015. http://www.theguardian.com/film/2012/may/18/ danny-glover-good-cop.

Joseph, Peniel E. "Haiti's revolt inspired US black activists." CNN, January 27, 2010. Accessed November 13, 2015. http://www.cnn.com/2010/ OPINION/01/26/joseph.african.americans.haiti/.

Laffita, Graciela Chailloux. "The Black Jacobins: Teachers of Revolution." *Caminos* 48 (2008). Accessed November 13, 2015. http://www.normangirvan. info/wp-content/uploads/2009/03/the-black-jacobins-graciela-challoux2.pdf.

Malik, Kenan. *The Meaning of Race*: *Race, History, and Culture in Western Society*. New York: New York University Press, 1996.

"C. L. R. James: The Black Jacobins." Kenan Malik, August 17, 2010. Accessed November 13, 2015, http://www.kenanmalik.com/reviews/james_jacobins.html.

Marx, Karl. *The German Ideology* (written 1845–6, published 1932). *Marxists*. Accessed November 13, 2015. https://www.marxists.org/archive/marx/ works/1845/german-ideology/ch01a.htm.

"The Eighteenth Brumaire of Louis Bonaparte." *Die Revolution* (1852). Accessed January 21, 2016. https://www.marxists.org/archive/marx/works/1852/18th-brumaire/ch01.htm

McNally, David. "E. P. Thompson: Class Struggle and Historical Materialism." *International Socialism Journal* 61 (1993). Accessed November 13, 2015. http://pubs.socialistreviewindex.org.uk/isj61/mcnally.htm.

Meeks, Brian. "Rereading *The Black Jacobins*: James, the Dialectic and the Revolutionary Conjuncture." *Social and Economic Studies* 43, no. 3 (1994).

Nielson, Aldon Lynn. *C. L. R. James: A Critical Introduction*. Jackson: University Press of Mississippi, 2010.

Norton, Justin M. "Q&A: Michael Gira of Swans on *To Be Kind*, Proper Crowdfunding, and the Human Voice." *Stereogum*, May 7, 2014. Accessed November 14, 2015. http://www.stereogum.com/1678536/qa-michael-gira-of-swans-on-to-be-kind-proper-crowdfunding-and-the-human-voice/franchises/interview/.

Ortiz, Paul. "C. L. R. James's Visionary Legacy." *Solidarity* (January/February 2012). Accessed November 13, 2015. http://www.solidarity-us.org/site/node/3494#R3.

Panaram, Sasha. "Toussaint: The Heartbeat of Freedom." *Black Atlantic*, March 6, 2004. Accessed November 14, 2015. http://sites.duke.edu/blackatlantic/2014/03/06/toussaint-the-heartbeat-of-freedom/#_ftn1.

Poyen-Bellisle, Henri de. *Histoire Militaire de la Révolution de Saint-Domingue*. Paris: Imprimerie Nationale, 1899.

Smith, Ashley. "The Black Jacobins." *International Socialist Review* 63. Accessed January 21, 2016. http://isreview.org/issue/63/black-jacobins

Stoddart, Brian. *Sport, Culture and History: Region, Nation and Globe*. New York: Routledge, 2013.

Sunder Rajan, Rajeswari. "Concepts in Postcolonial Theory: The Subaltern; and the Postcolonial Intellectual." New York University. Accessed November 13, 2015. http://english.fas.nyu.edu/docs/IO/7316/G41.2900(001)SunderRajanSyllabus.pdf.

Thompson, E. P. *The Making of the English Working Class*. London: Victor Gollancz, 1963.

Trotsky, Leon. "If America Should Go Communist." *Marxists*, August 1934. Accessed November 13, 2015. https://www.marxists.org/archive/trotsky/1934/08/ame.htm.

Walker, Corey. "Cross-currents in the African Diaspora." University of Virginia, 2004. Accessed November 13, 2015. http://www.virginia.edu/woodson/courses/aas102/syllabus2004.html.

Western Michigan University. "The Black Jacobins." *Colonial & Postcolonial Literary Dialogues* (April 16, 2001). Accessed November 13, 2015. http://wmich.edu/dialogues/texts/blackjacobins.html.

Williams, Carol J. "Where the Arab Spring Revolutions Went Wrong." *Los Angeles Times*, October 9, 2015. Accessed November 13, 2015. http://www.latimes.com/world/middleeast/la-fg-arab-spring-recap-hml-20151009-htmlstory.html.

Zartman, I. William, ed. *Arab Spring: Negotiating in the Shadow of the Intifadat*. Athens: University of Georgia Press, 2015.

THE MACAT LIBRARY
BY DISCIPLINE

The Macat Library By Discipline

AFRICANA STUDIES

Chinua Achebe's *An Image of Africa: Racism in Conrad's Heart of Darkness*
W. E. B. Du Bois's *The Souls of Black Folk*
Zora Neale Huston's *Characteristics of Negro Expression*
Martin Luther King Jr's *Why We Can't Wait*
Toni Morrison's *Playing in the Dark: Whiteness in the American Literary Imagination*

ANTHROPOLOGY

Arjun Appadurai's *Modernity at Large: Cultural Dimensions of Globalisation*
Philippe Ariès's *Centuries of Childhood*
Franz Boas's *Race, Language and Culture*
Kim Chan & Renée Mauborgne's *Blue Ocean Strategy*
Jared Diamond's *Guns, Germs & Steel: the Fate of Human Societies*
Jared Diamond's *Collapse: How Societies Choose to Fail or Survive*
E. E. Evans-Pritchard's *Witchcraft, Oracles and Magic Among the Azande*
James Ferguson's *The Anti-Politics Machine*
Clifford Geertz's *The Interpretation of Cultures*
David Graeber's *Debt: the First 5000 Years*
Karen Ho's *Liquidated: An Ethnography of Wall Street*
Geert Hofstede's *Culture's Consequences: Comparing Values, Behaviors, Institutes and Organizations across Nations*
Claude Lévi-Strauss's *Structural Anthropology*
Jay Macleod's *Ain't No Makin' It: Aspirations and Attainment in a Low-Income Neighborhood*
Saba Mahmood's *The Politics of Piety: The Islamic Revival and the Feminist Subjec*t
Marcel Mauss's *The Gift*

BUSINESS

Jean Lave & Etienne Wenger's *Situated Learning*
Theodore Levitt's *Marketing Myopia*
Burton G. Malkiel's *A Random Walk Down Wall Street*
Douglas McGregor's *The Human Side of Enterprise*
Michael Porter's *Competitive Strategy: Creating and Sustaining Superior Performance*
John Kotter's *Leading Change*
C. K. Prahalad & Gary Hamel's *The Core Competence of the Corporation*

CRIMINOLOGY

Michelle Alexander's *The New Jim Crow: Mass Incarceration in the Age of Colorblindness*
Michael R. Gottfredson & Travis Hirschi's *A General Theory of Crime*
Richard Herrnstein & Charles A. Murray's *The Bell Curve: Intelligence and Class Structure in American Life*
Elizabeth Loftus's *Eyewitness Testimony*
Jay Macleod's *Ain't No Makin' It: Aspirations and Attainment in a Low-Income Neighborhood*
Philip Zimbardo's *The Lucifer Effect*

ECONOMICS

Janet Abu-Lughod's *Before European Hegemony*
Ha-Joon Chang's *Kicking Away the Ladder*
David Brion Davis's *The Problem of Slavery in the Age of Revolution*
Milton Friedman's *The Role of Monetary Policy*
Milton Friedman's *Capitalism and Freedom*
David Graeber's *Debt: the First 5000 Years*
Friedrich Hayek's *The Road to Serfdom*
Karen Ho's *Liquidated: An Ethnography of Wall Street*

John Maynard Keynes's *The General Theory of Employment, Interest and Money*
Charles P. Kindleberger's *Manias, Panics and Crashes*
Robert Lucas's *Why Doesn't Capital Flow from Rich to Poor Countries?*
Burton G. Malkiel's *A Random Walk Down Wall Street*
Thomas Robert Malthus's *An Essay on the Principle of Population*
Karl Marx's *Capital*
Thomas Piketty's *Capital in the Twenty-First Century*
Amartya Sen's *Development as Freedom*
Adam Smith's *The Wealth of Nations*
Nassim Nicholas Taleb's *The Black Swan: The Impact of the Highly Improbable*
Amos Tversky's & Daniel Kahneman's *Judgment under Uncertainty: Heuristics and Biases*
Mahbub Ul Haq's *Reflections on Human Development*
Max Weber's *The Protestant Ethic and the Spirit of Capitalism*

FEMINISM AND GENDER STUDIES

Judith Butler's *Gender Trouble*
Simone De Beauvoir's *The Second Sex*
Michel Foucault's *History of Sexuality*
Betty Friedan's *The Feminine Mystique*
Saba Mahmood's *The Politics of Piety: The Islamic Revival and the Feminist Subject*
Joan Wallach Scott's *Gender and the Politics of History*
Mary Wollstonecraft's *A Vindication of the Rights of Woman*
Virginia Woolf's *A Room of One's Own*

GEOGRAPHY

The Brundtland Report's *Our Common Future*
Rachel Carson's *Silent Spring*
Charles Darwin's *On the Origin of Species*
James Ferguson's *The Anti-Politics Machine*
Jane Jacobs's *The Death and Life of Great American Cities*
James Lovelock's *Gaia: A New Look at Life on Earth*
Amartya Sen's *Development as Freedom*
Mathis Wackernagel & William Rees's *Our Ecological Footprint*

HISTORY

Janet Abu-Lughod's *Before European Hegemony*
Benedict Anderson's *Imagined Communities*
Bernard Bailyn's *The Ideological Origins of the American Revolution*
Hanna Batatu's *The Old Social Classes And The Revolutionary Movements Of Iraq*
Christopher Browning's *Ordinary Men: Reserve Police Batallion 101 and the Final Solution in Poland*
Edmund Burke's *Reflections on the Revolution in France*
William Cronon's *Nature's Metropolis: Chicago And The Great West*
Alfred W. Crosby's *The Columbian Exchange*
Hamid Dabashi's *Iran: A People Interrupted*
David Brion Davis's *The Problem of Slavery in the Age of Revolution*
Nathalie Zemon Davis's *The Return of Martin Guerre*
Jared Diamond's *Guns, Germs & Steel: the Fate of Human Societies*
Frank Dikotter's *Mao's Great Famine*
John W Dower's *War Without Mercy: Race And Power In The Pacific War*
W. E. B. Du Bois's *The Souls of Black Folk*
Richard J. Evans's *In Defence of History*
Lucien Febvre's *The Problem of Unbelief in the 16th Century*
Sheila Fitzpatrick's *Everyday Stalinism*

The Macat Library By Discipline

Eric Foner's *Reconstruction: America's Unfinished Revolution, 1863-1877*
Michel Foucault's *Discipline and Punish*
Michel Foucault's *History of Sexuality*
Francis Fukuyama's *The End of History and the Last Man*
John Lewis Gaddis's *We Now Know: Rethinking Cold War History*
Ernest Gellner's *Nations and Nationalism*
Eugene Genovese's *Roll, Jordan, Roll: The World the Slaves Made*
Carlo Ginzburg's *The Night Battles*
Daniel Goldhagen's *Hitler's Willing Executioners*
Jack Goldstone's *Revolution and Rebellion in the Early Modern World*
Antonio Gramsci's *The Prison Notebooks*
Alexander Hamilton, John Jay & James Madison's *The Federalist Papers*
Christopher Hill's *The World Turned Upside Down*
Carole Hillenbrand's *The Crusades: Islamic Perspectives*
Thomas Hobbes's *Leviathan*
Eric Hobsbawm's *The Age Of Revolution*
John A. Hobson's *Imperialism: A Study*
Albert Hourani's *History of the Arab Peoples*
Samuel P. Huntington's *The Clash of Civilizations and the Remaking of World Order*
C. L. R. James's *The Black Jacobins*
Tony Judt's *Postwar: A History of Europe Since 1945*
Ernst Kantorowicz's *The King's Two Bodies: A Study in Medieval Political Theology*
Paul Kennedy's *The Rise and Fall of the Great Powers*
Ian Kershaw's *The "Hitler Myth": Image and Reality in the Third Reich*
John Maynard Keynes's *The General Theory of Employment, Interest and Money*
Charles P. Kindleberger's *Manias, Panics and Crashes*
Martin Luther King Jr's *Why We Can't Wait*
Henry Kissinger's *World Order: Reflections on the Character of Nations and the Course of History*
Thomas Kuhn's *The Structure of Scientific Revolutions*
Georges Lefebvre's *The Coming of the French Revolution*
John Locke's *Two Treatises of Government*
Niccolò Machiavelli's *The Prince*
Thomas Robert Malthus's *An Essay on the Principle of Population*
Mahmood Mamdani's *Citizen and Subject: Contemporary Africa And The Legacy Of Late Colonialism*
Karl Marx's *Capital*
Stanley Milgram's *Obedience to Authority*
John Stuart Mill's *On Liberty*
Thomas Paine's *Common Sense*
Thomas Paine's *Rights of Man*
Geoffrey Parker's *Global Crisis: War, Climate Change and Catastrophe in the Seventeenth Century*
Jonathan Riley-Smith's *The First Crusade and the Idea of Crusading*
Jean-Jacques Rousseau's *The Social Contract*
Joan Wallach Scott's *Gender and the Politics of History*
Theda Skocpol's *States and Social Revolutions*
Adam Smith's *The Wealth of Nations*
Timothy Snyder's *Bloodlands: Europe Between Hitler and Stalin*
Sun Tzu's *The Art of War*
Keith Thomas's *Religion and the Decline of Magic*
Thucydides's *The History of the Peloponnesian War*
Frederick Jackson Turner's *The Significance of the Frontier in American History*
Odd Arne Westad's *The Global Cold War: Third World Interventions And The Making Of Our Times*

LITERATURE

Chinua Achebe's *An Image of Africa: Racism in Conrad's Heart of Darkness*
Roland Barthes's *Mythologies*
Homi K. Bhabha's *The Location of Culture*
Judith Butler's *Gender Trouble*
Simone De Beauvoir's *The Second Sex*
Ferdinand De Saussure's *Course in General Linguistics*
T. S. Eliot's *The Sacred Wood: Essays on Poetry and Criticism*
Zora Neale Huston's *Characteristics of Negro Expression*
Toni Morrison's *Playing in the Dark: Whiteness in the American Literary Imagination*
Edward Said's *Orientalism*
Gayatri Chakravorty Spivak's *Can the Subaltern Speak?*
Mary Wollstonecraft's *A Vindication of the Rights of Women*
Virginia Woolf's *A Room of One's Own*

PHILOSOPHY

Elizabeth Anscombe's *Modern Moral Philosophy*
Hannah Arendt's *The Human Condition*
Aristotle's *Metaphysics*
Aristotle's *Nicomachean Ethics*
Edmund Gettier's *Is Justified True Belief Knowledge?*
Georg Wilhelm Friedrich Hegel's *Phenomenology of Spirit*
David Hume's *Dialogues Concerning Natural Religion*
David Hume's *The Enquiry for Human Understanding*
Immanuel Kant's *Religion within the Boundaries of Mere Reason*
Immanuel Kant's *Critique of Pure Reason*
Søren Kierkegaard's *The Sickness Unto Death*
Søren Kierkegaard's *Fear and Trembling*
C. S. Lewis's *The Abolition of Man*
Alasdair MacIntyre's *After Virtue*
Marcus Aurelius's *Meditations*
Friedrich Nietzsche's *On the Genealogy of Morality*
Friedrich Nietzsche's *Beyond Good and Evil*
Plato's *Republic*
Plato's *Symposium*
Jean-Jacques Rousseau's *The Social Contract*
Gilbert Ryle's *The Concept of Mind*
Baruch Spinoza's *Ethics*
Sun Tzu's *The Art of War*
Ludwig Wittgenstein's *Philosophical Investigations*

POLITICS

Benedict Anderson's *Imagined Communities*
Aristotle's *Politics*
Bernard Bailyn's *The Ideological Origins of the American Revolution*
Edmund Burke's *Reflections on the Revolution in France*
John C. Calhoun's *A Disquisition on Government*
Ha-Joon Chang's *Kicking Away the Ladder*
Hamid Dabashi's *Iran: A People Interrupted*
Hamid Dabashi's *Theology of Discontent: The Ideological Foundation of the Islamic Revolution in Iran*
Robert Dahl's *Democracy and its Critics*
Robert Dahl's *Who Governs?*
David Brion Davis's *The Problem of Slavery in the Age of Revolution*

The Macat Library By Discipline

Alexis De Tocqueville's *Democracy in America*
James Ferguson's *The Anti-Politics Machine*
Frank Dikotter's *Mao's Great Famine*
Sheila Fitzpatrick's *Everyday Stalinism*
Eric Foner's *Reconstruction: America's Unfinished Revolution, 1863-1877*
Milton Friedman's *Capitalism and Freedom*
Francis Fukuyama's *The End of History and the Last Man*
John Lewis Gaddis's *We Now Know: Rethinking Cold War History*
Ernest Gellner's *Nations and Nationalism*
David Graeber's *Debt: the First 5000 Years*
Antonio Gramsci's *The Prison Notebooks*
Alexander Hamilton, John Jay & James Madison's *The Federalist Papers*
Friedrich Hayek's *The Road to Serfdom*
Christopher Hill's *The World Turned Upside Down*
Thomas Hobbes's *Leviathan*
John A. Hobson's *Imperialism: A Study*
Samuel P. Huntington's *The Clash of Civilizations and the Remaking of World Order*
Tony Judt's *Postwar: A History of Europe Since 1945*
David C. Kang's *China Rising: Peace, Power and Order in East Asia*
Paul Kennedy's *The Rise and Fall of Great Powers*
Robert Keohane's *After Hegemony*
Martin Luther King Jr.'s *Why We Can't Wait*
Henry Kissinger's *World Order: Reflections on the Character of Nations and the Course of History*
John Locke's *Two Treatises of Government*
Niccolò Machiavelli's *The Prince*
Thomas Robert Malthus's *An Essay on the Principle of Population*
Mahmood Mamdani's *Citizen and Subject: Contemporary Africa And The Legacy Of Late Colonialism*
Karl Marx's *Capital*
John Stuart Mill's *On Liberty*
John Stuart Mill's *Utilitarianism*
Hans Morgenthau's *Politics Among Nations*
Thomas Paine's *Common Sense*
Thomas Paine's *Rights of Man*
Thomas Piketty's *Capital in the Twenty-First Century*
Robert D. Putman's *Bowling Alone*
John Rawls's *Theory of Justice*
Jean-Jacques Rousseau's *The Social Contract*
Theda Skocpol's *States and Social Revolutions*
Adam Smith's *The Wealth of Nations*
Sun Tzu's *The Art of War*
Henry David Thoreau's *Civil Disobedience*
Thucydides's *The History of the Peloponnesian War*
Kenneth Waltz's *Theory of International Politics*
Max Weber's *Politics as a Vocation*
Odd Arne Westad's *The Global Cold War: Third World Interventions And The Making Of Our Times*

POSTCOLONIAL STUDIES

Roland Barthes's *Mythologies*
Frantz Fanon's *Black Skin, White Masks*
Homi K. Bhabha's *The Location of Culture*
Gustavo Gutiérrez's *A Theology of Liberation*
Edward Said's *Orientalism*
Gayatri Chakravorty Spivak's *Can the Subaltern Speak?*

PSYCHOLOGY

Gordon Allport's *The Nature of Prejudice*
Alan Baddeley & Graham Hitch's *Aggression: A Social Learning Analysis*
Albert Bandura's *Aggression: A Social Learning Analysis*
Leon Festinger's *A Theory of Cognitive Dissonance*
Sigmund Freud's *The Interpretation of Dreams*
Betty Friedan's *The Feminine Mystique*
Michael R. Gottfredson & Travis Hirschi's *A General Theory of Crime*
Eric Hoffer's *The True Believer: Thoughts on the Nature of Mass Movements*
William James's *Principles of Psychology*
Elizabeth Loftus's *Eyewitness Testimony*
A. H. Maslow's *A Theory of Human Motivation*
Stanley Milgram's *Obedience to Authority*
Steven Pinker's *The Better Angels of Our Nature*
Oliver Sacks's *The Man Who Mistook His Wife For a Hat*
Richard Thaler & Cass Sunstein's *Nudge: Improving Decisions About Health, Wealth and Happiness*
Amos Tversky's *Judgment under Uncertainty: Heuristics and Biases*
Philip Zimbardo's *The Lucifer Effect*

SCIENCE

Rachel Carson's *Silent Spring*
William Cronon's *Nature's Metropolis: Chicago And The Great West*
Alfred W. Crosby's *The Columbian Exchange*
Charles Darwin's *On the Origin of Species*
Richard Dawkin's *The Selfish Gene*
Thomas Kuhn's *The Structure of Scientific Revolutions*
Geoffrey Parker's *Global Crisis: War, Climate Change and Catastrophe in the Seventeenth Century*
Mathis Wackernagel & William Rees's *Our Ecological Footprint*

SOCIOLOGY

Michelle Alexander's *The New Jim Crow: Mass Incarceration in the Age of Colorblindness*
Gordon Allport's *The Nature of Prejudice*
Albert Bandura's *Aggression: A Social Learning Analysis*
Hanna Batatu's *The Old Social Classes And The Revolutionary Movements Of Iraq*
Ha-Joon Chang's *Kicking Away the Ladder*
W. E. B. Du Bois's *The Souls of Black Folk*
Émile Durkheim's *On Suicide*
Frantz Fanon's *Black Skin, White Masks*
Frantz Fanon's *The Wretched of the Earth*
Eric Foner's *Reconstruction: America's Unfinished Revolution, 1863-1877*
Eugene Genovese's *Roll, Jordan, Roll: The World the Slaves Made*
Jack Goldstone's *Revolution and Rebellion in the Early Modern World*
Antonio Gramsci's *The Prison Notebooks*
Richard Herrnstein & Charles A Murray's *The Bell Curve: Intelligence and Class Structure in American Life*
Eric Hoffer's *The True Believer: Thoughts on the Nature of Mass Movements*
Jane Jacobs's *The Death and Life of Great American Cities*
Robert Lucas's *Why Doesn't Capital Flow from Rich to Poor Countries?*
Jay Macleod's *Ain't No Makin' It: Aspirations and Attainment in a Low Income Neighborhood*
Elaine May's *Homeward Bound: American Families in the Cold War Era*
Douglas McGregor's *The Human Side of Enterprise*
C. Wright Mills's *The Sociological Imagination*

The Macat Library By Discipline

Thomas Piketty's *Capital in the Twenty-First Century*
Robert D. Putman's *Bowling Alone*
David Riesman's *The Lonely Crowd: A Study of the Changing American Character*
Edward Said's *Orientalism*
Joan Wallach Scott's *Gender and the Politics of History*
Theda Skocpol's *States and Social Revolutions*
Max Weber's *The Protestant Ethic and the Spirit of Capitalism*

THEOLOGY

Augustine's *Confessions*
Benedict's *Rule of St Benedict*
Gustavo Gutiérrez's *A Theology of Liberation*
Carole Hillenbrand's *The Crusades: Islamic Perspectives*
David Hume's *Dialogues Concerning Natural Religion*
Immanuel Kant's *Religion within the Boundaries of Mere Reason*
Ernst Kantorowicz's *The King's Two Bodies: A Study in Medieval Political Theology*
Søren Kierkegaard's *The Sickness Unto Death*
C. S. Lewis's *The Abolition of Man*
Saba Mahmood's *The Politics of Piety: The Islamic Revival and the Feminist Subject*
Baruch Spinoza's *Ethics*
Keith Thomas's *Religion and the Decline of Magic*

COMING SOON

Chris Argyris's *The Individual and the Organisation*
Seyla Benhabib's *The Rights of Others*
Walter Benjamin's *The Work Of Art in the Age of Mechanical Reproduction*
John Berger's *Ways of Seeing*
Pierre Bourdieu's *Outline of a Theory of Practice*
Mary Douglas's *Purity and Danger*
Roland Dworkin's *Taking Rights Seriously*
James G. March's *Exploration and Exploitation in Organisational Learning*
Ikujiro Nonaka's *A Dynamic Theory of Organizational Knowledge Creation*
Griselda Pollock's *Vision and Difference*
Amartya Sen's *Inequality Re-Examined*
Susan Sontag's *On Photography*
Yasser Tabbaa's *The Transformation of Islamic Art*
Ludwig von Mises's *Theory of Money and Credit*

Macat Disciplines

Access the greatest ideas and thinkers across entire disciplines, including

Postcolonial Studies

Roland Barthes's *Mythologies*
Frantz Fanon's *Black Skin, White Masks*
Homi K. Bhabha's *The Location of Culture*
Gustavo Gutiérrez's *A Theology of Liberation*
Edward Said's *Orientalism*
Gayatri Chakravorty Spivak's *Can the Subaltern Speak?*

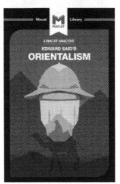

Macat analyses are available from all good bookshops and libraries.

Access hundreds of analyses through one, multimedia tool.
Join free for one month **library.macat.com**

Macat Disciplines

Access the greatest ideas and thinkers across entire disciplines, including

AFRICANA STUDIES

Chinua Achebe's *An Image of Africa: Racism in Conrad's Heart of Darkness*

W. E. B. Du Bois's *The Souls of Black Folk*

Zora Neale Hurston's *Characteristics of Negro Expression*

Martin Luther King Jr.'s *Why We Can't Wait*

Toni Morrison's *Playing in the Dark: Whiteness in the American Literary Imagination*

Macat analyses are available from all good bookshops and libraries.

Access hundreds of analyses through one, multimedia tool.

Join free for one month **library.macat.com**

Macat Disciplines

Access the greatest ideas and thinkers across entire disciplines, including

FEMINISM, GENDER AND QUEER STUDIES

Simone De Beauvoir's
The Second Sex

Michel Foucault's
History of Sexuality

Betty Friedan's
The Feminine Mystique

Saba Mahmood's
*The Politics of Piety:
The Islamic Revival and
the Feminist Subject*

Joan Wallach Scott's
*Gender and the
Politics of History*

Mary Wollstonecraft's
*A Vindication of the
Rights of Woman*

Virginia Woolf's
A Room of One's Own

Judith Butler's
Gender Trouble

Macat Disciplines

Access the greatest ideas and thinkers across entire disciplines, including

CRIMINOLOGY

Michelle Alexander's
*The New Jim Crow:
Mass Incarceration in the
Age of Colorblindness*

**Michael R. Gottfredson
& Travis Hirschi's**
A General Theory of Crime

Elizabeth Loftus's
Eyewitness Testimony

**Richard Herrnstein
& Charles A. Murray's**
*The Bell Curve: Intelligence and
Class Structure in American Life*

Jay Macleod's
*Ain't No Makin' It:
Aspirations and Attainment in a
Low-Income Neighborhood*

Philip Zimbardo's
The Lucifer Effect

Macat analyses are available from all good bookshops and libraries.

Access hundreds of analyses through one, multimedia tool.

Join free for one month **library.macat.com**

Macat Disciplines

Access the greatest ideas and thinkers across entire disciplines, including

INEQUALITY

Ha-Joon Chang's, *Kicking Away the Ladder*

David Graeber's, *Debt: The First 5000 Years*

Robert E. Lucas's, *Why Doesn't Capital Flow from Rich To Poor Countries?*

Thomas Piketty's, *Capital in the Twenty-First Century*

Amartya Sen's, *Inequality Re-Examined*

Mahbub Ul Haq's, *Reflections on Human Development*

Macat Disciplines

Access the greatest ideas and thinkers across entire disciplines, including

GLOBALIZATION

Arjun Appadurai's, *Modernity at Large: Cultural Dimensions of Globalisation*

James Ferguson's, *The Anti-Politics Machine*

Geert Hofstede's, *Culture's Consequences*

Amartya Sen's, *Development as Freedom*

Macat analyses are available from all good bookshops and libraries.

Access hundreds of analyses through one, multimedia tool.

Join free for one month **library.macat.com**

Macat Disciplines

Access the greatest ideas and thinkers across entire disciplines, including

THE FUTURE OF DEMOCRACY

Robert A. Dahl's, *Democracy and Its Critics*
Robert A. Dahl's, *Who Governs?*
Alexis De Toqueville's, *Democracy in America*
Niccolò Machiavelli's, *The Prince*
John Stuart Mill's, *On Liberty*
Robert D. Putnam's, *Bowling Alone*
Jean-Jacques Rousseau's, *The Social Contract*
Henry David Thoreau's, *Civil Disobedience*

Macat Disciplines

Access the greatest ideas and thinkers across entire disciplines, including

TOTALITARIANISM

Sheila Fitzpatrick's, *Everyday Stalinism*
Ian Kershaw's, *The "Hitler Myth"*
Timothy Snyder's, *Bloodlands*

Macat analyses are available from all good bookshops and libraries.

Access hundreds of analyses through one, multimedia tool.
Join free for one month **library.macat.com**

Macat Pairs

*Analyse historical and modern issues from opposite sides of an argument.
Pairs include:*

RACE AND IDENTITY

Zora Neale Hurston's
Characteristics of Negro Expression

Using material collected on anthropological expeditions to the South, Zora Neale Hurston explains how expression in African American culture in the early twentieth century departs from the art of white America. At the time, African American art was often criticized for copying white culture. For Hurston, this criticism misunderstood how art works. European tradition views art as something fixed. But Hurston describes a creative process that is alive, ever-changing, and largely improvisational. She maintains that African American art works through a process called 'mimicry'—where an imitated object or verbal pattern, for example, is reshaped and altered until it becomes something new, novel—and worthy of attention.

Frantz Fanon's
Black Skin, White Masks

Black Skin, White Masks offers a radical analysis of the psychological effects of colonization on the colonized.

Fanon witnessed the effects of colonization first hand both in his birthplace, Martinique, and again later in life when he worked as a psychiatrist in another French colony, Algeria. His text is uncompromising in form and argument. He dissects the dehumanizing effects of colonialism, arguing that it destroys the native sense of identity, forcing people to adapt to an alien set of values—including a core belief that they are inferior. This results in deep psychological trauma.

Fanon's work played a pivotal role in the civil rights movements of the 1960s.

Macat analyses are available from all good bookshops and libraries.

Access hundreds of analyses through one, multimedia tool.
Join free for one month **library.macat.com**

Macat Pairs

Analyse historical and modern issues from opposite sides of an argument. Pairs include:

INTERNATIONAL RELATIONS IN THE 21ST CENTURY

Samuel P. Huntington's
The Clash of Civilisations

In his highly influential 1996 book, Huntington offers a vision of a post-Cold War world in which conflict takes place not between competing ideologies but between cultures. The worst clash, he argues, will be between the Islamic world and the West: the West's arrogance and belief that its culture is a "gift" to the world will come into conflict with Islam's obstinacy and concern that its culture is under attack from a morally decadent "other."

Clash inspired much debate between different political schools of thought. But its greatest impact came in helping define American foreign policy in the wake of the 2001 terrorist attacks in New York and Washington.

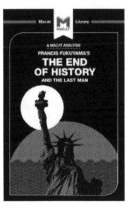

Francis Fukuyama's
The End of History and the Last Man

Published in 1992, *The End of History and the Last Man* argues that capitalist democracy is the final destination for all societies. Fukuyama believed democracy triumphed during the Cold War because it lacks the "fundamental contradictions" inherent in communism and satisfies our yearning for freedom and equality. Democracy therefore marks the endpoint in the evolution of ideology, and so the "end of history." There will still be "events," but no fundamental change in ideology.

Macat Pairs

Analyse historical and modern issues from opposite sides of an argument. Pairs include:

HOW TO RUN AN ECONOMY

John Maynard Keynes's
The General Theory OF Employment, Interest and Money

Classical economics suggests that market economies are self-correcting in times of recession or depression, and tend toward full employment and output. But English economist John Maynard Keynes disagrees.

In his ground-breaking 1936 study *The General Theory*, Keynes argues that traditional economics has misunderstood the causes of unemployment. Employment is not determined by the price of labor; it is directly linked to demand. Keynes believes market economies are by nature unstable, and so require government intervention. Spurred on by the social catastrophe of the Great Depression of the 1930s, he sets out to revolutionize the way the world thinks

Milton Friedman's
The Role of Monetary Policy

Friedman's 1968 paper changed the course of economic theory. In just 17 pages, he demolished existing theory and outlined an effective alternate monetary policy designed to secure 'high employment, stable prices and rapid growth.'

Friedman demonstrated that monetary policy plays a vital role in broader economic stability and argued that economists got their monetary policy wrong in the 1950s and 1960s by misunderstanding the relationship between inflation and unemployment. Previous generations of economists had believed that governments could permanently decrease unemployment by permitting inflation—and vice versa. Friedman's most original contribution was to show that this supposed trade-off is an illusion that only works in the short term.

Macat analyses are available from all good bookshops and libraries.

Access hundreds of analyses through one, multimedia tool.
Join free for one month **library.macat.com**

Macat Pairs

*Analyse historical and modern issues
from opposite sides of an argument.
Pairs include:*

ARE WE FUNDAMENTALLY GOOD - OR BAD?

Steven Pinker's
The Better Angels of Our Nature

Stephen Pinker's gloriously optimistic 2011 book argues that, despite humanity's biological tendency toward violence, we are, in fact, less violent today than ever before. To prove his case, Pinker lays out pages of detailed statistical evidence. For him, much of the credit for the decline goes to the eighteenth-century Enlightenment movement, whose ideas of liberty, tolerance, and respect for the value of human life filtered down through society and affected how people thought. That psychological change led to behavioral change—and overall we became more peaceful. Critics countered that humanity could never overcome the biological urge toward violence; others argued that Pinker's statistics were flawed.

Philip Zimbardo's
The Lucifer Effect

Some psychologists believe those who commit cruelty are innately evil. Zimbardo disagrees. In *The Lucifer Effect*, he argues that sometimes good people do evil things simply because of the situations they find themselves in, citing many historical examples to illustrate his point. Zimbardo details his 1971 Stanford prison experiment, where ordinary volunteers playing guards in a mock prison rapidly became abusive. But he also describes the tortures committed by US army personnel in Iraq's Abu Ghraib prison in 2003—and how he himself testified in defence of one of those guards. committed by US army personnel in Iraq's Abu Ghraib prison in 2003—and how he himself testified in defence of one of those guards.

Macat analyses are available from all good bookshops and libraries.

Access hundreds of analyses through one, multimedia tool.
Join free for one month **library.macat.com**

Macat Pairs

Analyse historical and modern issues from opposite sides of an argument. Pairs include:

HOW WE RELATE TO EACH OTHER AND SOCIETY

Jean-Jacques Rousseau's
The Social Contract

Rousseau's famous work sets out the radical concept of the 'social contract': a give-and-take relationship between individual freedom and social order.

If people are free to do as they like, governed only by their own sense of justice, they are also vulnerable to chaos and violence. To avoid this, Rousseau proposes, they should agree to give up some freedom to benefit from the protection of social and political organization. But this deal is only just if societies are led by the collective needs and desires of the people, and able to control the private interests of individuals. For Rousseau, the only legitimate form of government is rule by the people.

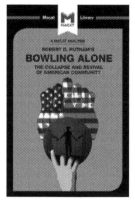

Robert D. Putnam's
Bowling Alone

In *Bowling Alone*, Robert Putnam argues that Americans have become disconnected from one another and from the institutions of their common life, and investigates the consequences of this change.

Looking at a range of indicators, from membership in formal organizations to the number of invitations being extended to informal dinner parties, Putnam demonstrates that Americans are interacting less and creating less "social capital" – with potentially disastrous implications for their society.

It would be difficult to overstate the impact of *Bowling Alone*, one of the most frequently cited social science publications of the last half-century.

Printed in the United States
by Baker & Taylor Publisher Services